The Sneaky Square

& Other Math Activities for Kids

Expanded 2nd Edition

Dr. Richard M. Sharp
Dr. Seymour Metzner

Illustrations by Steve Hoeft

TAB Books
An imprint of McGraw-Hill

New York San Francisco Washington, D.C. Auckland Bogotá
Caracas Lisbon London Madrid Mexico City Milan
Montreal New Delhi San Juan Singapore
Sydney Tokyo Toronto

McGraw-Hill

A Division of The McGraw·Hill Companies

©1996 by **The McGraw-Hill Companies, Inc.**
Published by TAB Books, an imprint of McGraw-Hill

pbk   1 2 3 4 5 6 7 8 9 0   DOC/DOC   9 0 0 9 8 7 6 5

Library of Congress Cataloging-in-Publication Data
ISBN   0-07-057232-1

McGraw-Hill books are available at special quantity discounts to use as premiums and sales promotions, or for use in corporate training programs. For more information, please write to the Director of Special Sales, McGraw-Hill, 11 West 19th Street, New York, NY 10011. Or contact your local bookstore.

Acquisitions editors: Kimberly S. Tabor
                 Judith Terrill-Breuer
Editorial team: Joanne Slike, Executive Editor
              Susan W. Kagey, Editor
Production team: Katherine G. Brown, Director
               Jan Fisher, Coding
               Jan Fisher, Desktop Operator
               Linda M. Cramer, Proofreading
               Joann Woy, Indexer
Design team: Jaclyn J. Boone, Designer
             Katherine Lukaszewicz, Associate Designer

0572321
SIES

Contents

Part 5 Positioning

Part 6 Mathematic Relationships

.... **Part 7 Calcutricks** ....

Introduction

The Sneaky Square and Other Math Activities for Kids—Expanded Second Edition is designed to arouse children's interest in mathematical activities, provide practice in basic number operations, and encourage creative approaches to solving problems.

The range of activities appeals to children at many grade levels and of differing abilities and backgrounds. The upper-level math problems should challenge the most apt students, while the less difficult activities will intrigue younger students. Many motivational learning procedures have been introduced to reinforce regular classroom mathematics curriculum. These have been proven effective in classroom settings from third to eighth grade.

The 25 additions to this revised edition of *The Sneaky Square and Other Math Activities for Kids* expand the mathematical vision of the original activities. The new activities are more interactive and concentrate on developing greater sophistication to problem-solving and higher levels of analytical logic.

The activities in Part 1, "Traps and Conundrums," mostly require typical computational skills with trial-and-error reasoning. This type of reasoning is the least challenging way to approach all problem-solving and was surely the main method used by our earliest ancestors. It is still a primary ingredient of scientific thinking. Thomas Edison's inventions and Paul Ehrlich's medical discoveries depended to a large degree on trial-and-error experimentation. Mathematically, trial-and-error can lead to a more intuitive understanding of algebra. These problems also highlight a need for looking beyond the obvious and seeking deeper and more complex levels of understanding.

The "Number Problems" in Part 2 call for an understanding of the decimal number system together with the mental flexibility to continually readjust hypotheses in dealing with widely varying and unique situations.

"Geometricks," Part 3, emphasizes reasoning and spatial relationships. This part should be particularly helpful to girls, who often do not get enough practice in these areas. Psychologists feel a lack of familiarity with these skills may be a reason for the underrepresentation of women in architecture and engineering.

The "Combination Puzzles" in Part 4 are exercises in creative ingenuity. They encourage insightful recognition of possibilities inherent in the recombination of preexisting elements. An example of this type thinking was what saved the astronauts of the Apollo 13 moon flight when their command module malfunctioned.

The "Positioning" exercises in Part 5 often call for the ability to generate multiple solutions. This practice is essential in helping students realize that real-life problems are often multidimensional, and they shouldn't always be satisfied with conventional, set solutions.

The "Mathematical Relationships" problems in Part 6 sharpen the mental faculties in using logical analysis and orderly thinking. Generating hypotheses and subjecting them to inductive and deductive verification are essential in science and mathematics. This part also promotes a greater appreciation of the interrelationships of all elements of the number system.

The last part, "Calcutricks," takes advantage of the ubiquitous presence of calculators in modern classrooms to advance familiarity and motivate creative experimentation in their use. Teachers can also take advantage of these exercises to emphasize the importance of approximation and estimation to check on machine-generated answers. This is an important antidote to the misconception that any answer coming from a machine *must* be correct!

The nature of mathematical thinking is such that, although each part seeks to develop specific skills and understandings, conceptual elements from other parts are also utilized. Such synergistic interactions are integral to intellectual processes.

I
ESP

Difficulty Level: Medium
Materials: Paper, pencils

Tell . . . . Show

I will demonstrate that I have a
sixth sense. Follow these
directions:

Write down any two numbers
from 1 to 9.

3, 7

Multiply either number by 5.

$5 \times 3 = 15$

Add 3 to your answer.

$15 + 3 = 18$

Double the sum you just wrote.

$18 \times 2 = 36$

Add to it the other number you
started with.

$36 + 7 = 43$

When I call on you, tell me your
final number, and I will tell you
your two original numbers.

Subtracting 6 gives you a number
with the two original digits.

$(43 - 6 = 37 = 3, 7)$

. . . . Explanation . . . .

This demonstration depends on algebraic manipulations. Multiplying by 5
and later doubling was really multiplying by 10. Adding 3 became adding 6
with this doubling. In effect, subtracting 6 undid the adding of 6, and
separating the answer into individual digits undid the multiplying by 10.

2
X-Ray

Difficulty Level: Medium
Materials: None

Tell . . . . Show

I will now show the class I have X-ray vision and can see through your bodies.

Tear off two small pieces of paper. Write 1¢ on one piece and 10¢ on the other.

Place a piece in each hand and close your fist. Remember which one is in your left hand and which one is in your right hand.

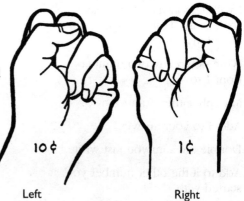

Left   Right

Multiply what's in your right hand by 4. Remember the answer.

$$1¢ \times 4 = 4¢$$

Multiply what's in your left hand by 3. (5 or 7 may also be used.)

Keep this number in your head.

$$3 \times 10¢ = 30¢$$

Add together the two numbers in your head.

$$30¢ + 4¢ = 34¢$$

When I call on you, tell me the answer and I'll tell you which hand has which coin.

If the answer is an even number, the penny is in the right hand. If odd, it's in the left hand.

. . . . Explanation . . . .

This trick is based on elementary number theory, which says that adding two even numbers results in an even number and adding an odd number and an even number produces an odd number. The multiplication with the right hand always results in an even number, whereas the number generated by the left hand will be either even or odd depending on the coin in it.

3
E Pluribus Unum

Difficulty Level: Medium
Materials: Paper, pencils

Tell . . . . Show

Write any two numbers from 50 to 100.

65, 83

Add them.

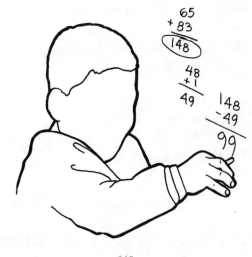

Cross out the first digit on the left.

1̷48

Add one to the remaining number.

48 + 1 = 49

Subtract this new number from your original sum. What is your answer?

148
− 49
─────
99

The answer will always be 99.

. . . . Explanation . . . .

This series of steps is related to casting out nines, which is inherent in our number system. The sum of the digits in the subtraction is always 18.

4
Ditto

Difficulty Level: High
Materials: Paper, pencils

Tell . . . . Show

I will ask one of you to pick your
favorite number from 1 to 9.
Write it on the board, and work
on the board together with the
class.

7

Write the number I am putting on
the board. Notice there is no 8 in
this number.

Multiply this number by the
number given by the pupil (in
this example, 7).

$$1\,2\,3\,4\,5\,6\,7\,9$$
$$1\,2\,3\,4\,5\,6\,7\,9$$
$$\times\,7$$
$$\overline{8\,6\,4\,1\,9\,7\,5\,3}$$

Multiply your new number by 9.

$$8\,6\,4\,1\,9\,7\,5\,3$$
$$\times\,9$$
$$\overline{}$$

What is your answer?

$$7\,7\,7\,7\,7\,7\,7\,7\,7$$

. . . . Explanation . . . .

This is a number oddity in which the sum of the digits in every answer is
always a multiple of nine. In this example, multiplying by 7 and then by 9
was, in effect, multiplying by 63, which generated an answer of all 7's,
whose sum of digits is 63.

5
Presto

Difficulty Level: Medium
Materials: Paper, pencils

Tell .... Show

I will write a magic number on a piece of paper, fold it, and ask Carol to hold it tightly in her hand.

Ann, write a three-digit number on the board using three different digits.

478

Jack, write another three-digit number right under Ann's.

478
539

Since you have written two numbers, I will also write 2 numbers.

521
460

Add these four numbers.

478
539
521
+ 460
_____
1998

Carol, read the magic number on
the paper you're holding.   1998

············· Explanation ·············

The sum is always 1998. Each number the teacher writes must be added to
a pupil's number so that the pair equals 999 as in the diagram:

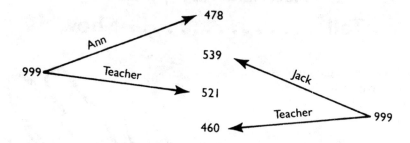

Therefore, you have two 999s, or the sum of 1998.

6
Speed Demon

Difficulty Level: High
Materials: Paper, pencils

Tell . . . . Show

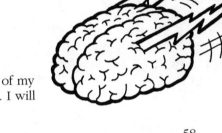

I will give you an example of my lightning-fast brain at work. I will ask one of you to write a problem on the board multiplying a two-digit number by another two-digit number.

$$\begin{array}{r} 58 \\ \times\ 23 \\ \hline \end{array}$$

I will write a second problem on the board. [The teacher writes the same multiplicand (top number) as the pupil, but the multiplier (bottom number) is the difference between 23 and 99 (99 − 23 = 76).]

$$\begin{array}{r} 58 \\ \times\ 76 \\ \hline \end{array}$$

The class will now do these two multiplication problems, add together the answers, and see if anyone can get the total before I do it in my head.

Teacher note: Your bottom number (multiplier) is found by subtracting the pupil's bottom number from 99.

Answer: 5742. Subtracting 1 from the top number (58) gives 57, the first 2 digits of the answer, while subtracting the top number (58) from 100 gives the 42, the last 2 digits of the answer.

5742

.... Explanation ....

This shortcut involves the distributive property of multiplication over subtraction and also is linked to casting out nines. In our example, we are multiplying ninety-nine (23 + 76) 58s, but instead, to make things easier, we are multiplying one hundred 58s by simply annexing two zeros to 58 (5800). Because we substituted 100 for 99, we have to subtract a 58 from 5800 (5800 − 58) which gives the correct answer: 5742.

7
Add-Along

Difficulty Level: Medium
Materials: Paper, pencils

Tell . . . . Show

I will ask someone to put any number from 1 to 9 on the board.

I will write some more numbers to make an addition problem.

(Every number is 3 more than the preceding number. Any sequence of numbers can be used as long as there is the same amount of increase between them. This challenge works best using an even number of terms.)

We'll see if anyone in the class can add these numbers on his or her paper before I do it in my head.

Answer: 124. In this example, the answer is obtained by adding the top and bottom numbers (5 + 26 = 31). Then count up the number of terms (8). Divide the number of terms in half (½ of 8 = 4) and multiply that number by the previous sum (4 × 31 = 124).

```
  5

  5
  8
 11
 14
 17
 20
 23
 26
 ──
```

. . . . Explanation . . . .

This problem involves an informal method for determining arithmetic sums.

8
Payday

Difficulty Level: Medium
Materials: Paper, pencils

Tell . . . . Show

Pretend you are offered an executive position by a billionaire who asks you to choose which one of two ways you prefer to be paid. The first way, you would receive 1¢ for the first day. Each day your pay would be doubled, for 31 days a month. The second day you receive 2¢, the third day 4¢, the fourth day 8¢, and so on.

$1,000 + $2,000 + $3,000 + $4,000, etc., after 31 days would amount to nearly a half million dollars ($496,000).

The other way is to receive $1,000 the first day and an additional thousand dollars every succeeding day. This way you will receive $2,000 the second day, $3,000 the third day, $4,000 the fourth day and so on. Which method of payment would you prefer?

1¢ + 2¢ + 4¢ + 8¢, etc., after 31 days would total more than 20 million dollars!

. . . . Explanation . . . .

This situation involves comparing the sum of an arithmetic sequence (1,000 + 2,000 + 3,000 + ...) and the sum of a geometric sequence (1¢ + 2¢ + 4¢ + ...). The doubling effect of a geometric sequence gallops along and rapidly overtakes any arithmetic sequence.

9
Card Shark

Difficulty Level: Medium
Materials: Paper, pencils, playing cards (deck)

Tell . . . . Show

Here's a famous Las Vegas card trick. I will call on volunteers to do simple calculations on the board while I face away from the board.

Sue, pick any card from this deck and write both its value and suit on the board. An ace is one, a jack is 11, a queen is 12, and a king is 13. Cards 2 to 10 keep their face value.

♠ = 4

♡ = 3

◇ = 2

♣ = 1

Juan, double the value of the card.

$9 \times 2 = 18$

Billie Joe, add 2 to Juan's answer.

$18 + 2 = 20$

Victoria, multiply Billie Joe's answer by 5.

$5 \times 20 = 100$

Hank, look at the suit number chart on the board, and add the correct suit number to Victoria's total. Tell me your answer.

$100 + 3 = 103$

The card Sue picked is the 9 of hearts.

Subtract 10 from the answer (103 −10 = 93), and the left-hand digit (or two digits) tells you the card value (9) and the right-hand digit is the suit value as shown on the chart (3 = hearts).

·············· Explanation ··············

This manipulation involves algebraic reasoning, but is easier to explain in arithmetic terms. Multiplying the card value moves it to the tens place or the hundreds place, and you have an extra 10. Subtracting 10 undoes this operation. Adding the suit value (1, 2, 3, or 4) places it in the one's column.

10
Tisket Tasket Basket

Difficulty Level: Low
Materials: None

Tell . . . . Show

If I had six pieces of candy to share among three children, how many should each get?

Two candies apiece

A mother baked nine brownies to share among nine Cub Scouts. How could each scout get one but still have one brownie left in the bag?

One scout gets the ninth brownie in the bag.

. . . . Explanation . . . .

The solutions to many problems depend on examining hidden premises.

II
California Express

Difficulty Level: Low
Materials: None

Tell . . . . Show

The California Express leaves Los Angeles for San Francisco traveling at 90 mph, while at the same time, the Pacific Limited leaves San Francisco for Los Angeles, traveling 60 mph. When the trains meet, which one is nearer Los Angeles?

They are equidistant from Los Angeles.

. . . . Explanation . . . .

Since when they meet they are at the same place, their speed of travel is immaterial, and they are at the same distance from any location.

12
St. Ives

Difficulty Level: Low
Materials: None

Tell . . . . Show

As I was going to St. Ives, I met a man with seven wives. Every wife had seven sacks. Every sack had seven cats. Every cat had seven kits. Kits, cats, sacks, and wives; how many were going to St. Ives?

One

. . . . Explanation . . . .

Only the narrator was going to St. Ives. To meet people on the road means they are going in opposite or different directions. This is a traditional puzzle.

13
Bird Brains

Difficulty Level: Low
Materials: None

Tell . . . . Show

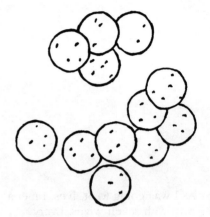

Jane brought 12 cookies to class.
She gave away four of them.
How many were left?

Answer: 8

A farmer saw 11 crows on a
fence. He shot three of them.
How many remained?

Answer: 3

.... **Explanation** ....

Only the three dead crows remained, because the others flew away.

14
Special Sale

Difficulty Level: Medium
Materials: None

Tell . . . . Show

A new homeowner bought something that cost:

    1 for $1.00
    12 for $2.00
    144 for $3.00

What item could reasonably account for this pricing?

Write "1" on the board.
Write "12" on the board.
Write "144" on the board.
Answer: House numbers

. . . . Explanation . . . .

We ordinarily consider numbers as representations of definite quantities. A problem that treats numbers as digits, ignoring place value, creates distractive ambiguity. Ambiguity in mathematical language arises when we confuse numbers with symbols. In the above example, we think of 144 as a quantity, of 144 things (number) rather than as three separate digits or items worth $1 each.

15
Midas Touch

Difficulty Level: Medium
Materials: None

Tell . . . . Show

Which would you rather have:
4 pounds of $10 silver coins
or 2 pounds of $20 silver coins?
Explain your answer.

Answer: 4 pounds of $10 coins

. . . . Explanation . . . .

A heavier weight would always be worth more than a lighter weight of the same matter, in this case silver. The worth of each individual coin is irrelevant because worth is dependent on total weight.

16
Tight Fist

Difficulty Level: Low
Materials: Coins

Tell . . . . Show

I have three coins in my hand. They add up to 45¢. What are the coins?

Answer: 1 quarter, 2 dimes

I now have three other coins in my hand. They total 85¢. One is *not* a dime. What are the coins?

Answer: Half dollar, quarter, dime

·············· **Explanation** ··············

Saying *one* is not a dime doesn't mean one of the other two can't be. This example demonstrates drawing unwarranted inferences from a false premise.

17
Dead of Night

Difficulty Level: Medium
Materials: None

Tell . . . . Show

A CIA agent's wife told me how her husband died of shock in his sleep. She said he dreamed he was captured and was about to be shot when a car backfired and the sudden noise killed him immediately. What is wrong with this story?

If the agent died without waking, how could his wife know what he was dreaming?

. . . . Explanation . . . .

Inferences based on false assumptions lead to erroneous conclusions.

18
What's Cooking?

Difficulty Level: Low
Materials: None

Tell . . . . Show

A 4-pound male turkey takes 80 minutes to cook, while a 4-pound female turkey takes 1 hour and 20 minutes to cook. What might account for the difference in cooking time?

There is no difference.
80 minutes = 1 hour, 20 minutes

. . . . Explanation . . . .

Pupils are often distracted by irrelevant information in thought problems.

19
Dating Game

Difficulty Level: Medium
Materials: None

Tell . . . . Show

A grasshopper on a number line jumps from negative 4 to positive 5, one number at a time. How many jumps did it make?

9 Jumps

-4 -3 -2 -1 0 1 2 3 4 5

A Roman child wrote on his pet's tombstone, "Here lies Fido, born 3 BC, died 4 AD." How old was Fido when he died?

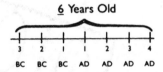

Explanation

The real number line has a zero. The calendar number line goes from 1 BC to 1 AD without a zero, so from 3 BC to 4 AD is only 6 spaces, or years, rather than 7, because there is no zero.

20
Post Office

Difficulty Level: Medium
Materials: None

Tell . . . . Show

If there are 3 feet in a yard, how many yards are in 12 feet?

$12 \div 3 = 4$ feet

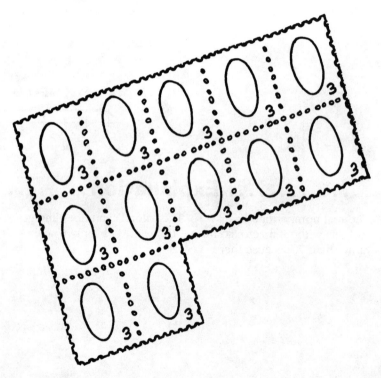

If there are 12 one-cent stamps in a dozen, how many three-cent stamps are in a dozen?

12

. . . . Explanation . . . .

By definition, a dozen of anything contains 12 items.

21
Ink Spots

Difficulty Level: High
Materials: None

Tell . . . . Show

A printer made so many errors on pages 14, 15, 79, 115, and 116 that he had to replace them. How many sheets of paper did he have to reprint?

Four sheets

. . . . Explanation . . . .

All books start with page 1 on the right-hand side. Page 2 is the other side of page 1. Any pair of consecutive pages starting with an odd number is one sheet of paper. Any pair of consecutive pages starting with an even number would be two sheets.

22
Hocus Pocus

Difficulty Level: High
Materials: Paper, pencils

Tell . . . . Show

Divide 100 by 25 and add 6.
What do you get?

$$100 \div 25 + 6 = 10$$

Divide 30 by ½ and add 10. What
is the answer?

$$(30 \div \text{½}) + 10 = 70$$

Most pupils will answer 25!

. . . . Explanation . . . .

When we do division, we are asking how many of the divisors can be taken
from the dividend. In this case, we are asking how many halves can be
taken from 30; the answer is 60 one-halves.

23
Crime Doesn't Pay

Difficulty Level: High
Materials: None

Tell . . . . Show

A shoplifter in a numismatist's (coin dealer's) store stole the oldest coin he could find, dated 279 BC. If a rare coin is worth $10 for each year before Christ that it was minted, how much could he sell it for?

Zero dollars

. . . . Explanation . . . .

The coin had to be counterfeit, because the term "BC" could not have been used then. "BC" means "before Christ," and the minter could not know Christ was going to be born 279 years after he minted the coin.

24
Neatza Pizza

Difficulty Level: High
Materials: Paper, pencils

Tell . . . . Show

A party of eight people ordered a large pizza like the one on the board. The waiter, a real show-off, divided it into 8 equal pieces with only 3 straight cuts of his knife. On your paper, show how he did it.

1st cut (Divide in half)

2nd cut (Divide in quarters)

3rd cut

(The four quarter pieces are stacked and sliced down the middle to make 8 pieces)

. . . . Explanation . . . .

The maximum number of pieces you can make with two cuts is four. Any third cut in the same plane can make no more than seven pieces. Therefore, a two-dimensional solution doesn't work, and we must look for a third dimension solution, namely stacking the pieces.

25
Gibberish

Difficulty Level: Medium
Materials: Paper, pencils

Tell . . . . Show

Unscramble each of the phrases
on the board to form a familiar
math word.

a) Can it for
b) Cart tubs
c) Lumty lip
d) Me run B
e) Mad lice
f) I son vidi

a) fraction
b) subtract
c) multiply
d) number
e) decimal
f) division

. . . . Explanation . . . .

Decoding nonsense phrases can be difficult when they include rearranging
letters to form new words or sentences (anagrams).

26
Hazy Daze

Difficulty Level: Low
Materials: None

Tell . . . . Show

The alphabet has 26 letters. How
many are not vowels?

21

Some months have 30 days, some
have 31 days. How many have 28
days?

All of them (12)

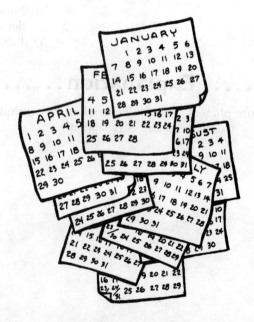

. . . . Explanation . . . .

Every month has at least 28 days, although February has only 28 days. The
question did not ask which month or months had only 28 days.

27
Tall Tale

Difficulty Level: Low
Materials: None

Tell . . . . Show

When Ann was five, her mother measured her against a tree and marked it at a height of 3 feet. If the tree grows 1 foot every year, how high would the mark be after 10 years?

3 feet

. . . . Explanation . . . .

A tree grows taller from its top, so the rest of the tree remains at the same height.

28
A Corny Tail

Difficulty Level: Low
Materials: None

Tell .... Show

Peter Rabbit ate two ears of corn every day for five days. How many ears did he eat altogether?

10 ears

Farmer Jones hid a dozen ears of corn in a box to keep them from Peter Rabbit. But Peter found the box, entered, and crawled out with three ears everyday. How long did it take to empty the box?

12 days!

.... **Explanation**.............

Although he left with three ears a day, two of those belonged to him (on his head), so he only took away one ear of corn daily.

29
Big Dig

Difficulty Level: Medium
Materials: None

Tell . . . . Show

If four men take six days to dig a ditch, how long will it take two men to dig a ditch half that size?

Six days. Since the men and the job are *both* reduced by half, there is no reason to change the time.

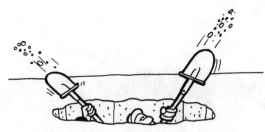

If two men can dig a hole in one day, how long will it take one man to dig half a hole?

You can't dig *half* a hole.

. . . . Explanation . . . .

Any hole you dig, by definition, is a complete hole. Since a hole can be thought of as zero (nothing), you can't have half of zero, or nothing.

30
Cavity

Difficulty Level: Medium
Materials: None

Tell . . . . Show

How many cubic feet of water can be removed from a hot tub 10 feet wide, 5 feet long, and 3 feet deep?

10 feet × 5 feet × 3 feet = 150 cubic feet

How much dirt can be removed from a hole that is 3 feet deep, 2 feet wide, and 10 feet long?

None

. . . . Explanation . . . .

By definition, a *hole* is a cavity with nothing in it. Therefore, there is nothing to be removed.

31
Topsy-Turvy

Difficulty Level: Low
Materials: Paper, pencils

Tell . . . . Show

What three-digit number, turned
upside down, spells a source of
energy?

710 = OIL

. . . . Explanation . . . .

Some digits have the configuration of letters when viewed from different
perspectives.

32
Tender Trap

Difficulty Level: Medium
Materials: None

Tell .... Show

I'll say a series of numbers. After each number, the whole class should immediately answer with the next higher number. For example, when I say *fourteen*, the whole class should respond by saying *fifteen*.

Class answers should be put on the board for effect.

Note: The class will almost certainly have been lured into answering *five* thousand. Discuss with them why they made the error.

Eight	9
Fifty-six	57
Thirty-two	33
One hundred sixty-five	166
Four hundred ninety-nine	500
Four thousand ninety-nine	4,100

.... Explanation ....

The students are trapped into the mistake of saying *five thousand* because the only place value signal they heard was thousand in *four thousand ninety-nine*.

33
Happy Birthday

Difficulty Level: Low
Materials: None

Tell . . . . Show

Dorothy is five years old. Tom is
four years old, and Jose is eight
years old. How many birthdays
have all these children had?

$$\begin{array}{r} 5 \\ 4 \\ 8 \\ \hline \end{array}$$

When the children call out the
answer "17," write down "3" as
the answer.

3

. . . . Explanation . . . .

A birthday is the day you were born. You might have celebrated it eight
times over eight years. but you still had only *one birthday*, namely the day
you were actually born.

34
Do or Die

Difficulty Level: Low
Materials: None

Tell . . . . Show

Your car breaks down in a blizzard, and you struggle through the snow to a cabin. It is freezing inside and you must get warm or die. You have only one match, and you see an oil lamp, a fireplace with wood, and a stove with coal in it. Which do you attempt to light first?

You light the match, of course!

. . . . Explanation . . . .

This example helps explain the difficulty in math word problems where operational priority is essential. The cabin problem is a classic case of misdirection where attention is fixed on combustible heat sources rather than the obvious first step necessary to ignite them.

35
Have you herd?

Difficulty Level: Low
Materials: Paper, pencils

Tell . . . . Show

I'll name individual items and what a group of them are called. Then I'll call on someone to tell me if I'm correct or to name the correct group. For example, "Do 2 male dolphins plus 7 female dolphins = a school?" The answer is "Yes" since a group of fish is a "school."

1. Do 3 cows and 5 bulls = a herd?

2. Do 6 baseball players and 3 baseball players = a team?

3. Do 1 tenor and 1 soprano = a quartet?

4. Do 3 inches and 9 inches = a foot?

5. Would 2 apples and 4 apples = a henway?

1. Yes

2. Yes

3. No. They are a duet. A quartet has four members.

4. Yes

5. Student: "What's a henway?"

   Teacher: "About 3 or 4 pounds, or pretty close to what a rooster weighs."

. . . . Explanation . . . .

Problem-solving is often difficult due to a rigid mindset. This example demonstrates the "lateral thinking" needed to approach a situation from a radically different angle.

36
Next!

Difficulty Level: Low
Materials: None

Tell . . . . Show

In the sequence of numbers on the board, what number should go into the top box?

In the sequence of letters on the board, what letter should go into the top box?

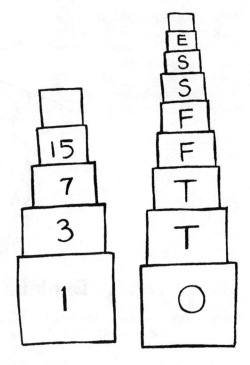

. . . . Explanation . . . .

In the first example, the answer is 31, because each number is double the previous number plus 1. The answer to the second example is "n". Each letter corresponds to the written number sequence *o*ne, *t*wo, *t*hree, *f*our, *f*ive, etc.

37
Rescue

Difficulty Level: Medium
Materials: None

Tell . . . . Show

Indiana Jones is stuck on a large rock in the middle of a pool filled with vicious, hungry piranhas. The nearest edge of the pool is 20 feet away from the rock. His father wants to rescue him, but he has only 2 planks, each 19½ feet long. How can he rescue his son?

. . . . Explanation . . . .

Logic dictates that more than one board must be used. One can't be used to extend the other since there's nothing around to join them, so one must be used as a base. This line of thinking leads directly to the solution since there's only one way for the edge of the pool to support a base.

38
Poison T

Difficulty Level: Medium
Materials: None

Tell . . . . Show

On the board are three rows of Ts. A class member and I, taking turns, may erase as many Ts as we wish from any *one* row. The next player may erase any of the remaining Ts on that row or any other row, but again from only one row. The loser is the one who is left with only *one* T to erase, the Poison T.

A) T T T T
B)   T T T T
C)   T T T

If you force your opponent into any of the following five positions on his or her turn, you will have a definite advantage:

1) T T
   T T

2) T T T
   T T T

3) T T T T
   T T T T

4) T
   T
   T

5) T T T ⎫
   T T   ⎬ in any order
   T   ⎭

. . . . Explanation . . . .

This game is a variation of the ancient game "Nim," which is based on reasoning in binary notation.

39
Candy Store

Difficulty Level: Medium
Materials: Paper, pencils

Tell . . . . Show

Suzy went to the candy store and brought home 100 pieces of candy, which cost exactly $1.00. On the board are the three kinds of candy she bought and their prices. How many of each kind did she buy?

10 ¢

5 ¢

2/1 ¢

Tootsie Roll   10¢ each
Peppermint sticks   5¢ each
Jelly beans   2 for 1¢

Answer:

1 Tootsie Roll	10¢
9 Peppermint sticks	45¢
90 Jelly beans	45¢
	$1.00

. . . . Explanation . . . .

Inductive thinking and trial-and-error experimentation solve this problem.

40
Blockade

Difficulty Level: Medium
Materials: Paper, pencils, marker

Tell . . . . Show

On the board are five numbers. Ann, stand in front of any number you want.

1 ▨ 3 4 5

I will now stand in front of another number and the class will add these two numbers together.

1 ▨ 3 4 ▨

Class responds "7."

Ann, please sit down. Jimmy, stand in front of any of the five numbers except the one I'm blocking. The class will now add this number to the previous total.

1 2 ▨ 4 ▨

Class responds "10."

I will now choose any of the five numbers except Jimmy's, and we will add this number to the previous total.

▨ 2 ▨ 4 5

Class responds "11."

We will continue in this manner until either a class member or I stands in front of a number that brings the total to 37. The person who stands in front of this number will be the winner. Anyone who brings the total over 37 automatically loses.

Whoever blocks any number that gets the total to 30 can force a "win." All the future moves after 30 are clear except when a pupil blocks "1." The teacher then must block "3," which guarantees a "win."

·············· **Explanation**··············

This exercise is an application of the maximum-minimum concept to calculus.

41
Carnival

Difficulty Level: Medium
Materials: Paper, pencils

Tell . . . . Show

A ring toss at a carnival advertises a grand prize for anyone who can total exactly 100 points with 10 tosses or less. More than one ring may be on a number. The numbered stakes are shown on the board.

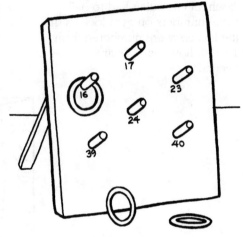

Answer:	Two 16s	=	32
	Four 17s	=	68
			100

. . . . Explanation . . . .

This problem combines addition with inferential thinking to arrive at the unique solution.

42
Lucky Seven

Difficulty Level: Medium
Materials: Paper, pencils

Tell . . . . Show

A school custodian had to nail metal numbers on gym lockers. If the lockers were numbered from 1 to 99, how many 7s are needed?

20 (7, 17, 27, 37, 47, 57, 67, 70, 71, 72, 73, 74, 75, 76, 77, 78, 79, 87, 97)
[Note that 77 requires *two* 7s.]

. . . . Explanation . . . .

A correct solution calls for care in visualizing place value.

43
Square Dance

Difficulty Level: Medium
Materials: Paper, pencils, scissors

Tell . . . . Show

Fold your paper into 16 parts.

[Teacher gives appropriate directions.]

Unfold the paper and number the squares as they are shown on the board. Write large. Cut out the 16 squares.

1	2	3	4
5	6	7	8
9	10	11	12
13	14	15	16

Arrange all these squares with 4 in each row and 4 in each column so each row and each column equals 34. The two diagonals going from corner to corner must also equal 34. An example of one of these is on the board. There are many others. When you find another solution, raise your hand. If it's correct, you may place your solution on the board. The rest of the class will seek other solutions.

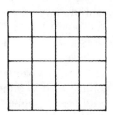

15	6	9	4	= 34
10	3	16	5	= 34
8	13	2	11	= 34
1	12	7	14	= 34

There are 880 solutions.

. . . . Explanation . . . .

This number sequence is called a 4-by-4 magic square. Any regular number sequence that can be placed in a square (3-by-3, 4-by-4, 5-by-5, etc.) can be arranged into a magic square.

44
Apache

Difficulty Level: Medium
Materials: Paper, pencils

Tell . . . . Show

Each of you should have a partner. On the board I have drawn nine dots arranged in a square. Draw these on your paper. Taking turns, one drawing and one watching, try to connect all the dots with four straight lines without lifting your pencil from the paper. You must not retrace a line, but you may cross over a line. Once you start you must complete the figure or it becomes your partner's turn.

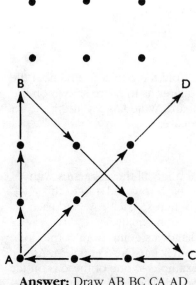

Answer: Draw AB BC CA AD

. . . . Explanation . . . .

The solution depends on not viewing the nine dots as the boundary of a closed figure, thereby forming a mindset that precludes a creative response.

45

Architect

Difficulty Level: High
Materials: Paper, pencils

Tell . . . . Show

Each of you should have a partner. On the board I have drawn a house. Taking turns, one drawing and the other watching, try to draw this figure in one continuous line without lifting your pencil off the paper. You must not retrace a line, but you may cross over a line. Once you start you must complete the figure or it becomes your partner's turn.

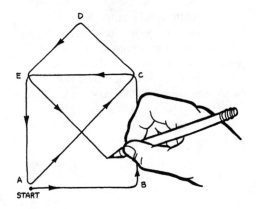

Answer: Draw AB BC CE EA AC CD DE EB

There are other solutions.

. . . . Explanation . . . .

In a topological puzzle similar to the above, you must start at one of the odd vertices and try to end at the other odd vertex. A and B are the odd vertices because they have 3 lines going to them.

46
Smarty

Difficulty Level: Low
Materials: None

Tell . . . . Show

I have written the numerals 1 to 9
on the board. I will take turns
with different students to choose
one of the numbers on the board.
I will circle my numbers and put
a triangle around the class
numbers. The winner is the first
one to get three numbers
totalling 15.

2	9	4
7	5	3
6	1	8

. . . . Explanation . . . .

The numbers make up a "magic square" of 15 in all directions. It's a
camouflaged tic-tac-toe game where the teacher can win or force a draw
since he or she knows beforehand all possible winning or drawing
sequences and can easily block any student play. The teacher can write the
square on a small slip of paper ahead of time and keep it handy for
reference.

47

Boa Constructor

Difficulty Level: Medium
Materials: Paper, pencils

Tell . . . . Show

Drawn on the board is a snake with its scales numbered from 1 to 25. Copy it onto your paper.

1. What three adjoining scales of the snake add up to 21?

   1. 6, 7, 8

2. What are the first two adjoining scales which, when added together and divided by 5 will equal 5?

   2. 12, 13

3. What are the first three adjoining scales of the snake the sum of which is exactly divisible by 8?

   3. 7, 8, 9

. . . . Explanation . . . .

It would be helpful to use calculators on these problems. They are examples of the combinatorial properties of our number system.

48
Slippery Squares

Difficulty Level: High
Materials: 12 crayons per team of two

Tell . . . . Show

Arrange your crayons in three touching squares as shown on the board.

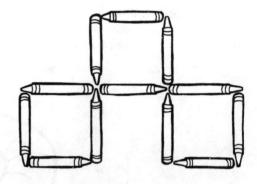

Change the positions of three of these crayons so that all the crayons now form five squares.

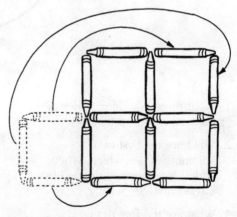

The fifth square is the entire figure, which contains the four smaller squares.

. . . . Explanation . . . .

The answer depends on having the minimum number of crayons on the perimeter. The most economical area is the one with the smallest perimeter.

49
Triple Threat

Difficulty Level: High
Materials: Paper, pencils

Tell .... Show

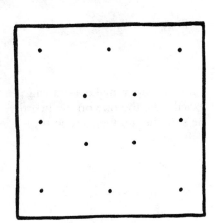

Draw a figure on your paper just like the one on the board.

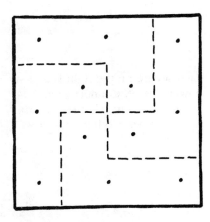

Divide the squares into four sections with each section containing three dots. The sections must be the same size and shape.

.... Explanation ....

The dot distribution calls for the square to be subdivided into congruent six-sided regions. Regular polygonal areas can be partitioned into an infinite number of irregular polygonal regions.

50
Short Circuit

Difficulty Level: High
Materials: Paper, pencils

Tell . . . . Show

On your paper, make a drawing exactly like the one on the board. Be sure the numbers are in the right places.

Each square on the right is a power source. Connect each power source to a house with the same number. No line may cross another line.

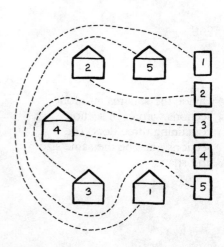

. . . . Explanation . . . .

The answer is dependent on the realization that the problem cannot be solved by simply using straight lines. Topological reasoning separates the surface interior and exterior regions.

51
Divide and Conquer

Difficulty Level: Medium
Materials: Pencil, paper,
straightedge ruler

Tell . . . . Show

Draw a four-sided figure similar
to the drawing on the board.

Draw four straight lines with each
line connecting two sides of the
figure. With these four lines, try
to make as many sections as
possible inside the figure. Use
your straightedge in drawing the
lines. The lines may cross each
other. You are allowed to try to
find a solution as many times as
you want.

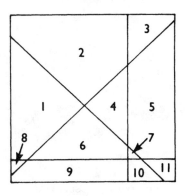

Answer: 11

. . . . Explanation . . . .

There is a maximum of 11 sections that can be drawn with four straight
lines. You create the maximum number of sections by having each line
intersect all other lines.

52
Sneaky Square

Difficulty Level: High
Materials: Paper, ruler,
pencils, scissors

Tell . . . . Show

Does everyone have on his or
her desk a pair of scissors, paper,
a ruler, and a pencil?

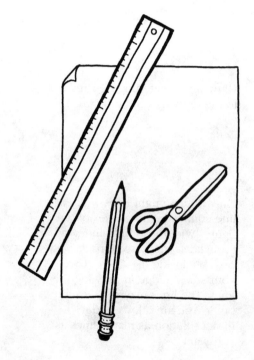

On the board you see a
rectangle. Its size is 2 inches
wide and 10 inches long. Copy
this rectangle on your paper. Be
sure all four corners make right
angles.

10″

2″

Place your ruler along the top line and put a dot at 4 inches and 8 inches. Do the same with the bottom line and connect the top and bottom dots.

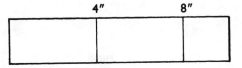

Draw 2 diagonal lines as they are on the board.

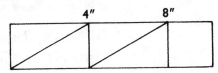

Letter each section as it is on the board.

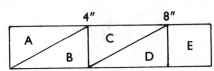

Cut out each lettered section and reassemble them into a perfect square with the letters showing.

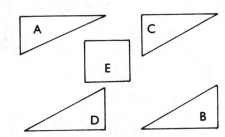

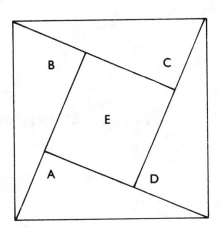

············· **Explanation**··············

Any rectangle can be transformed into a square. This dissection is a classical Greek approach to visualizing the Pythagorean theorem.

53
Tricky Ten

Difficulty Level: Medium
Materials: Crayons (15 per
team of two pupils

Tell .... Show

Using your crayons, form three
figures as they are shown on the
board.

From the three figures, remove a
total of six crayons so that ten
remains. Do not move any
others.

Answer: Remove the crayons
indicated by dotted lines and
those remaining will spell out the
number *TEN*.

.... Explanation ....

This manipulation illustrates the need for linguistic precision in expressing
mathematical ideas.

54
Fair Share

Difficulty Level: High
Materials: Paper, pencils, ruler

Tell . . . . Show

A home builder died and left land to his wife and four children. The land was shaped like a perfect square as shown on the board. One quarter of the land (Section A) was willed to his wife. The other three quarters was divided equally in size and shape among his four children.

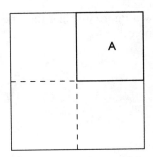

Draw a picture showing how his division was done. Remember each of the four sections must be the same size and shape.

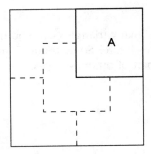

Answer: Divide the original square into fourths. One-fourth (Square A) was already willed to his wife. Since three squares were left to be subdivided among the four children, taking one-fourth of each of the remaining squares gives each child a congruent shape as shown in the diagram.

. . . . Explanation . . . .

Area relationships can be interpreted in arithmetic terms, and any area can be partitioned into congruent regions.

55
Triangle Trip

Difficulty Level: Medium
Materials: Paper, pencils

Tell . . . . Show

Draw a figure just like the one on the board.

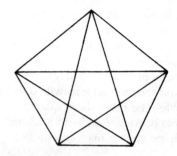

How many triangles can you find in this figure? Some triangles may be part of other triangles.

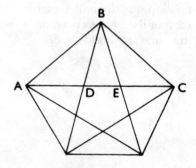

Answer: There are 35 triangles. Examples are ABD, BEC, AEB, BDE, etc. Anywhere there are intersections, the pupils should search for triangles.

. . . . Explanation . . . .

Polygonal shapes contain other polygonal shapes once the interior chords are drawn.

56
Tennis Menace

Difficulty Level: Medium
Materials: Paper, pencils

Tell . . . . Show

Draw a picture just like the one
on the board.

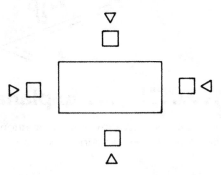

The center figure is a private
tennis court. Each triangle and
square is a house around the
court. All the people in the
triangular houses are allowed to
use the court because they paid
for a membership. The people in
the square houses must be kept
away from the court because they
haven't paid. Draw a fence
around the court so that all the
people in the triangular houses
can get to the court without
having to cross the fence, but it
keeps out the people in the
square houses.

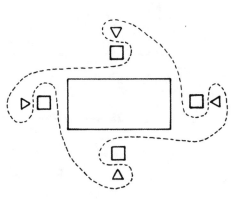

·············· Explanation ··············

Topological surfaces involving continuous paths require an insight into the relationship between interior and exterior spaces.

57

Wheel of Fortune

Difficulty Level: Low
Materials: Papers, pencils

Tell . . . . Show

On the board is a wheel subdivided into 9 sections. I will choose two players. One player is assigned Xs, and the other player is assigned Os. Taking turns, write a total of three Xs or three Os during your turn. Your three marks may be made within *one* section, or they may be written in *two* or *three* touching sections. The winner is the player who places a mark in the last empty section.

Sample game

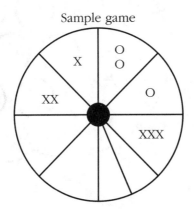

. . . . Explanation . . . .

This partner activity involves the use of strategic thinking based on the base-two system. The players must decide how to spread out their marks.

58
Flip-Flop

Difficulty Level: Medium
Materials: Markers
(beans, coins, etc.)

Tell . . . . Show

Arrange the 10 markers on your
desk to form a triangle as shown
on the board. Moving the fewest
markers, reverse the triangle so
that the top becomes the bottom
and vice versa.

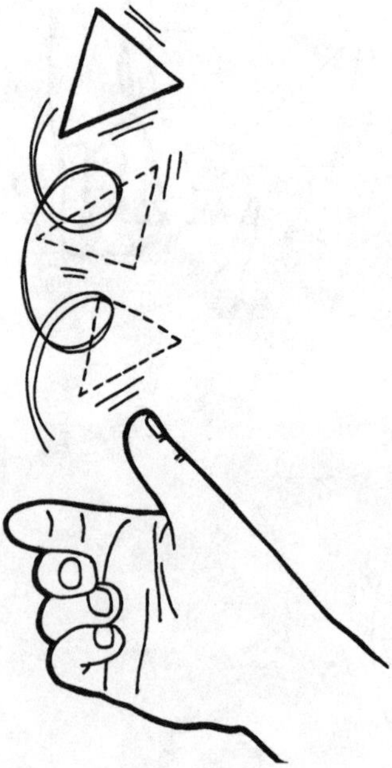

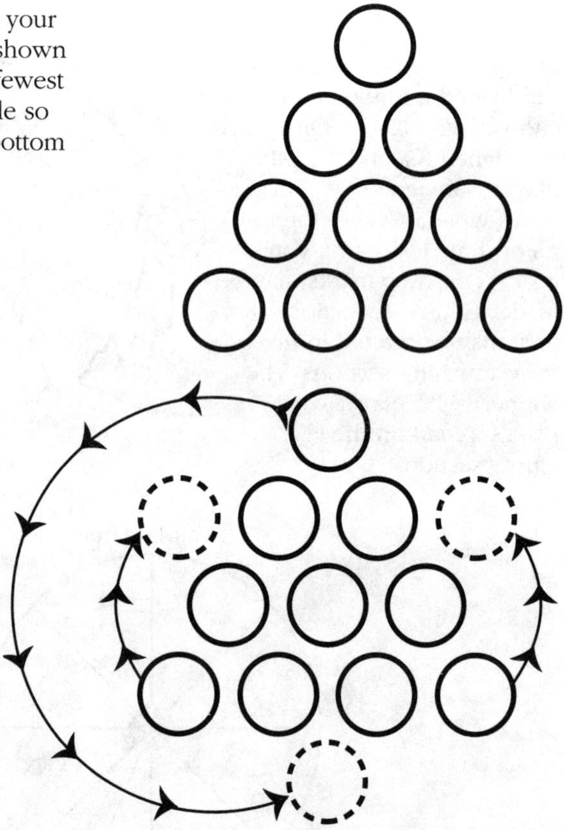

. . . . Explanation . . . .

This reversal problem calls for intuitive geometry leading to a mirror-image
solution.

59

Roisterous Roosters

Difficulty Level: High
Materials: Paper, pencils

Tell . . . . Show

Six quarrelsome roosters were
separated from each other by 13
individual lengths of fencing.
The farmer needed one of the
pieces for a fence post and
rearranged the remaining pieces
to form six enclosures of equal
size and shape. Illustrate on your
paper how the farmer rearranged
the fencing.

·············· Explanation ··············

This exercise in abstract geometrical reasoning requires conceptualization of shapes other than four-sided ones.

60
Millennium

Difficulty Level: High
Materials: Paper, pencils

Tell . . . . Show

The Denver Dodos, a baseball team, decided they'd like to change their lineup every day to improve their chances of winning. How long would it take before they had tried every possible lineup arrangement of their 9 players?

Almost 1,000 years! (994.19 to be exact)

. . . . Explanation . . . .

This is a permutation problem solved by the following factorial procedure:
9 × 8 × 7 × 6 × 5 × 4 × 3 × 2 × 1 = 362,880 days, or 994.19 years (362,888 ÷ 365).

61

Scramble

Difficulty Level: Medium
Materials: Paper, pencils

Tell . . . . Show

Arrange the digits 1 to 9 in a
3-by-3 square so that no number
has a smaller number following it
on the same row or anywhere
below it. One example of such a
square is on the board. See how
many of these arrangements you
can make. There are 42 possible
ways to arrange the digits.

```
1 3 6
2 5 7
4 8 9
```

. . . . Explanation . . . .

The top left number must always be 1 and the bottom right number must
always be 9. Once the pupils discern this pattern, other relationships will
become apparent. Five possible solutions are:

```
1 4 6    1 2 5    1 3 4    1 2 4    1 3 5
2 5 8    3 4 6    2 6 7    3 5 6    2 4 6
3 7 9    7 8 9    5 8 9    7 8 9    7 8 9
```

62
Match Up

Difficulty Level: High
Materials: Paper, pencils

Tell · · · · · · · · · · · · · Show

Five girls, Anne, Betty, Sally, Rhoda, and Karen, entered a Ping-Pong tournament, Each girl had to play the others once. In order to do this, how many matches must be played in all?

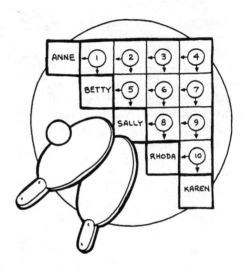

10 matches

· · · · · · · · · · · · Explanation · · · · · · · · · · · · ·

In an elementary combinational problem, it is best to analyze the problem by diagramming it as follows:

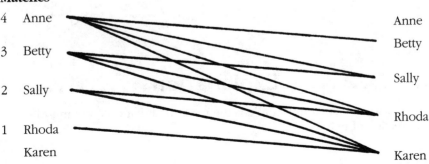

Matches

4 Anne

3 Betty

2 Sally

1 Rhoda

Karen

Anne

Betty

Sally

Rhoda

Karen

63
SOS

Difficulty Level: High
Materials: Paper, pencils

Tell . . . . Show

Arrange 10 dots in such a way that there are five lines with four dots in each line. The same dot may be used in two separate lines where the lines cross. In the example on the board, I have 10 dots in two lines. You must draw 10 dots in five lines, with four dots in each line.

Answer:

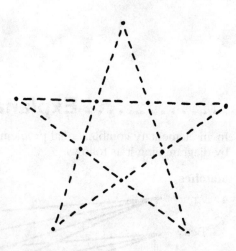

. . . . Explanation . . . .

The key to unlocking this puzzle is the realization that each dot must be the intersection of two lines.

64
Fill 'er Up

Difficulty Level: High
Materials: Paper, pencils

Tell . . . . Show

Make your paper exactly like the diagram on the board. Each box should be large enough to write a number in it.

$$\boxed{} - \boxed{} = \boxed{}$$
$$\times$$
$$\boxed{} \div \boxed{} = \boxed{}$$
$$\boxed{} + \boxed{} = \boxed{}$$

Using each number from 1 to 9 only once, fill in the squares so that all four equations are correct.

$$\boxed{9} - \boxed{5} = \boxed{4}$$
$$\times$$
$$\boxed{6} \div \boxed{3} = \boxed{2}$$
$$\boxed{1} + \boxed{7} = \boxed{8}$$

. . . . Explanation . . . .

The clue to solving this set of equations is to complete the multiplication and addition equations.

65
Gypsy

Difficulty Level: Medium
Materials: None

Tell .... Show

On the board I have put four magical crystal balls with numbers inside them.

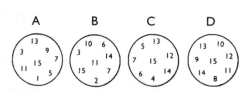

While my back is turned, I will ask one of you to choose a number from 1 to 15 and put it on the board so the class can see it.

9

Erase the letter above each crystal ball that has this number inside it. Now erase the number you wrote on the board.

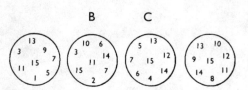

I will now face the crystal balls and tell you the number you originally chose.

Answer: 9

The sum of the bottom numbers in the circles whose letters were erased is always the answer. In this case letters A and D were erased, and their bottom numbers were 1 + 8 = 9.

.... Explanation ....

The numbers are placed in the circles according to binary notation. The target (bottom) numbers (1, 2, 4, 8) are all powers of two, and all the other numbers in that circle belong to the same power of two.

66
Las Vegas

Difficulty Level: Medium
Materials: Three dice

Tell . . . . Show

While my back is turned to the board, I will ask one of you to come to the desk, roll the three dice, and then stack them one on top of another as shown on the board. The pupil stacking them will then write on the board the number of dots on the bottom face of the die marked A (the top die), the top and bottom faces of B (the middle die), and the top and bottom faces of C (the bottom die). The three dice shall be returned to the same place in the stack. All five numbers should be added together on the board. After this, erase all the numbers on the board. I will turn around, look at the stacked dice with my magic eye, and tell you the secret sum you placed on the board.

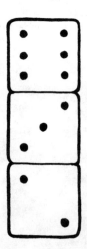

You always find the answer by subtracting the top face of the stack from 21. For example, if the top face had four dots, then 21 − 4 would give you 17, the secret sum.

. . . . Explanation . . . .

Opposite faces of a die always equal 7. With three stacked dice, there are three pairs of opposite faces, and three 7s equal 21. When you see the top face, subtract this visible part of the 21, which gives you the secret sum.

67

Wizard

Difficulty Level: Medium
Materials: Paper, pencils

Tell . . . . Show

I will show you that I am a
genuine mind reader. I'll call one
of you to work at the board
while I face the back of the
room. The rest of the class
should watch closely to see that
all directions have been followed
correctly. Do the following:

Write any three-digit number on
the board, using three different
digits.

186

Using the same digits, switch
them around in any way to make
another three-digit number.

861

Line up the larger number over
the smaller number.

861
186

Subtract the bottom number from
the top number.

861
− 186
‾‾‾‾‾
675

Erase everything except the
answer.

675

Erase one of the digits in the
answer and replace it with a box.

6 ☐ 5

I will now write the missing digit
in the mystery box.

6 7 5

Teacher: Add the digits that can be seen (6 + 5 = 11) and subtract this sum from the next multiple of nine (18 in this case) to get the missing digit (7). **Note:** If the seen digit or digits add exactly to a multiple of nine, the erased digit is nine (9).

············· Explanation ··············

This demonstration depends on the characteristics of our numeration system and is a reversal of casting out nines.

68
Wrong Number

Difficulty Level: Low
Materials: Paper, pencils

Tell . . . . Show

On the board is a picture of a touch-tone phone dial. Each button has several letters and a number linked with them. Based on these letters and numbers, answer the following questions:

1. Does "horse" or "tiger" have the greater value?
2. What flower has a value of 21?
3. What is the highest-value animal you can name?
4. What is the longest sentence you can write with every word having the same value?
5. Who has the highest-value first name in this class?

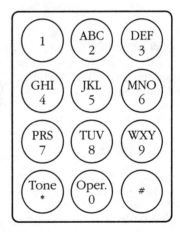

. . . . Explanation . . . .

In the first problem, "horse" has a greater value—the numbers add up to 27; "tiger" adds up to 26. The second answer is "lily." The other questions have open-ended, class-dependent answers. The class will enjoy making up problems for the rest of the students to answer.

69
Magic Apples

Difficulty Level: Medium
Materials: Paper, pencils

Tell . . . . Show

A grocer made a display of 28 apples around a table. He arranged them so that he could easily determine if any had been taken by checking that each side totalled 9 apples.

A thief came in, stole 4 apples, and rearranged the rest so that, when the grocer checked, he still had 9 on each side.

Later, another thief came in and took 4 more apples, rearranging the rest so that when the grocer checked he still counted 9 on each side. How did each of the two thieves rearrange the display?

·············· **Explanation**··············

Since each corner number is added twice (once horizontally and once vertically), taking 2 apples from each middle section and adding 1 of them to each corner number keeps the totals the same.

70
Chain Gang

Difficulty Level: Medium
Materials: Paper, pencils

Tell . . . . Show

On the board is an equation with operational signs missing. Copy the equation onto your paper. In each square, place either a plus or minus sign so the equation equals one.

1 ☐ 2 ☐ 3 ☐ 4 ☐ 5 ☐ 6 ☐ 7 ☐ 8 ☐ 9 = 1

1 ⊞ 2 ⊞ 3 ⊞ 4 ⊟ 5 ⊞ 6 ⊞ 7 ⊟ 8 ⊟ 9 = 1

There are other solutions.

. . . . Explanation . . . .

The sum of the numbers 1 through 9 equals 45. The ability to group numbers together to get a difference of one helps solve this equation.

71
Ship Shape

Difficulty Level: Medium
Materials: Paper, pencils

Tell . . . . Show

Draw a figure like the one on the board. Using every one of the digits from 4 to 9, place each one in a circle so that every side equals 21.

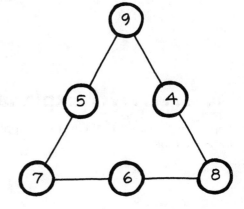

Draw a figure like the one on the board. Using every one of the digits from 1 to 11, place each one in a circle so that every straight line of three circles totals 18. The center circle is always used.

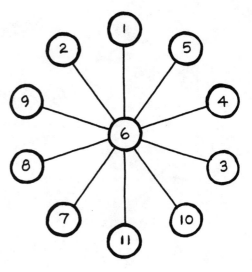

Draw a figure like the one on the board. Using every one of the digits from 1 to 12, place each in a circle so that each straight row of four circles adds up to 26.

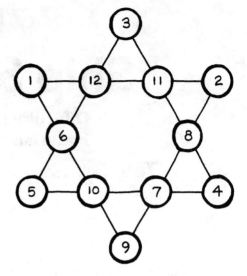

.... **Explanation** ....

Pupils must be able to discover overlapping number relationships to solve these patterns.

72
See Saw

Difficulty Level: Medium
Materials: Paper, pencils

Tell . . . . Show

Starting with a number from 1 to 10, build a number pattern using eight additional numbers. You build this pattern by adding the same amount to each succeeding number. Use any amount, but don't make the jumps between the neighboring numbers too large. A sample is on the board.

2, 5, 8, 11, 14, 17, 20, 23, 26

(each number jumps by 3)

Make a 3-by-3 square like the one on the board.

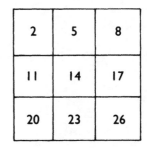

Fill it in with your numbers— the first three in the top squares, the next three in the middle squares, and the last three in the bottom squares.

2	5	8
11	14	17
20	23	26

Add all the numbers together and write their sum on your paper.

The answer will always be 9 times the center square. In the example above, 9 × 14 (the center square) = 126.

I will call on one of you to put your square on the board and then we'll see if anyone in the class who hasn't used the same number pattern can get the answer by using paper and pencil before I do it in my head.

.... Explanation ....

In any sequence or number pattern with an odd number of entries, the middle one divides the whole sequence into two parts so that the sum is found by multiplying the middle number (which is the average) by nine (the number of entries). Likewise, in a sequence with five entries, you would multiply the middle entry by five to get the sum of the sequence.

73
Bow Wow

Difficulty Level: Medium
Materials: Paper, pencils

Tell . . . . Show

In a pet shop, 10 dogs wore different tags numbered from 1 to 10. Two dogs apiece were placed in each of five kennels marked East, West, North, South, and Central Kennels. In each kennel, the numbers on the two dogs are added together. The total results are shown on the board. What pair of dogs were in each of the kennels? There are several solutions.

North Kennel   = 12
East Kennel   = 11
South Kennel   = 8
West Kennel   = 15
Central Kennel = 9

North	= 12	10, 2	8, 4	9, 3	10, 2	9, 3
East	= 11	7, 4	2, 9	10, 1	8, 3	7, 4
South	= 8	5, 3	7, 1	6, 2	7, 1	6, 2
West	= 15	9, 6	10, 5	8, 7	9, 6	10, 5
Central	= 9	1, 8	6, 3	4, 5	5, 4	1, 8

The pupils may find other solutions.

. . . . Explanation . . . .

This problem primarily uses the skills of renaming sums along with deductive reasoning.

74

Stop the Clock

Difficulty Level: Medium
Materials: Paper, pencils, and rulers

Tell . . . . Show

On the board you see the face of a clock. Draw a clock face on your paper and try to make two straight lines across it so that the clock numbers in each section add up to the same sum.

The sum of each section equals 26.

$$11 + 12 + 1 + 2 = 26$$
$$10 + 9 + 3 + 4 = 26$$
$$8 + 7 + 6 + 5 = 26$$

. . . . Explanation . . . .

The sum of the clock numbers is 78. Two intersecting lines always make 4 sections. Since 78 cannot be divided evenly into 4 sections, we must seek another solution: The lines must not intersect and the clock face must be divided into three sections.

75
Oddits

Difficulty Level: Medium
Materials: Paper, pencils

Tell . . . . Show

There are 11 ways of adding 8 odd numbers together to make 20. Numbers may be repeated. See how many of these you can get. An example labeled "A" is on the board.

A. $13 + 1 + 1 + 1 + 1 + 1 + 1 + 1$

B. $11 + 3 + 1 + 1 + 1 + 1 + 1 + 1$

C. $9 + 5 + 1 + 1 + 1 + 1 + 1 + 1$

D. $9 + 3 + 3 + 1 + 1 + 1 + 1 + 1$

E. $7 + 7 + 1 + 1 + 1 + 1 + 1 + 1$

F. $7 + 5 + 3 + 1 + 1 + 1 + 1 + 1$

G. $7 + 3 + 3 + 3 + 1 + 1 + 1 + 1$

H. $5 + 5 + 5 + 1 + 1 + 1 + 1 + 1$

I. $5 + 5 + 3 + 3 + 1 + 1 + 1 + 1$

J. $5 + 3 + 3 + 3 + 3 + 1 + 1 + 1$

K. $3 + 3 + 3 + 3 + 3 + 3 + 1 + 1$

. . . . Explanation . . . .

These equations may be solved once the pupils understand that adding two odd numbers results in an even number, and they can group numbers appropriately.

76
Sparkle

Difficulty Level: High
Materials: Paper, pencils

Tell . . . . Show

Three miners found diamonds weighing 5, 13, 12, 4, 9, 8, 15, 10, and 6 ounces apiece. They each found three. Each of Tom's diamonds weighed twice as much as Dick's. Which three diamonds did Harry find?

While there are several solutions if only the total weight of Tom's diamonds was twice the total weight of Dick's diamonds, there is only one solution in which each of Tom's diamonds weighed twice as much as one of Dick's diamonds:

5, 13, 12, 4, 9, 8, 15, 10, 6

Answer:

Tom:	8, 10, 12	= 30
Dick:	4, 5, 6	= 15
Harry:	9, 13, 15	= 37

. . . . Explanation . . . .

Although an algebraic equation could be used, most children will find the answer by using a trial-and-error procedure.

77

Castaway

Difficulty Level: High
Materials: Paper, pencils

Tell . . . . Show

Smokin' Sam was stranded on a desert island with just one box of 64 cigars. He wanted them to last as long as possible and found that by smoking exactly ¾ of each cigar, he could stick four butts together to make another whole cigar. How many extra cigars can he smoke by using this method?

21 extra cigars

. . . . Explanation . . . .

Sixty-four (64) original cigars leave 64 one-quarters (¼s). Putting together four of those one-quarters (¼s) makes another cigar, which amounts to 16 new cigars. There will be 16 one-quarters (¼s) left from these. These one-quarters (¼s) make four new whole cigars. The same process repeated with those four cigars gives one new cigar. The total new cigars would then be 21 (16 + 4 + 1).

78
Assembly Line

Difficulty Level: High
Materials: Paper, pencils

Tell . . . . Show

There are many ways of combining every one of the digits from 1 to 9 so that they equal 100. These digits, 1 to 9, must be arranged in order, and individual digits may be used together to form a number. Create as many similar equations as you can. Two examples are on the board.

$$1 + (2 \times 3) + 4 + 5 + (67) + 8 + 9 = 100$$

$$123 + 4 - 5 + 67 - 89 = 100$$

Some other solutions:

$$1 + 2 + 3 + 4 + 5 + 6 + 7 + (8 \times 9) = 100$$

$$(1 \times 2) + 34 + 56 + 7 - 8 + 9 = 100$$

$$12 + 3 - 4 + 5 + 67 + 8 + 9 = 100$$

$$123 - 45 - 67 + 89 = 100$$

$$1 + 2 + 3 - 4 + 5 + 6 + 78 + 9 = 100$$

. . . . Explanation . . . .

Success here depends upon the manipulation of numerical relationships.

79

Quatro

Difficulty Level: High
Materials: Paper, pencils

Tell . . . . Show

I will give you a target number from 0 to 20. You are to reach this number by writing an equation with just 4s. You can only use four 4s in your equation. You may use any operation (+, −, ×, ÷), decimals, and/or parentheses. If the target number was 3, an equation to reach 3 might be $(4 + 4 + 4) \div 4$. I will write this example on the board.

$$(4 + 4 + 4) \div 4 = 3$$

Answers:

$0 = 44 - 44$

$1 = (4 \div 4) \times (4 \div 4)$

$2 = (4 \div 4) + (4 \div 4)$

$3 = (4 + 4 + 4) \div 4$

$4 = 4 \times (4 - 4) + 4$

$5 = [(4 \times 4) + 4] \div 4$

$6 = 4 + [(4 + 4) \div 4]$

$7 = (4 + 4) - (4 \div 4)$

$8 = 4 + 4 + 4 - 4$

$9 = (4 + 4) + (4 \div 4)$

$10 = (44 - 4) \div 4$

$11 = (4 \div 4) + (4 \div .4)$

$12 = (44 + 4) \div 4$

$13 = 4 + [(4 - .4) \div .4]$

$14 = [4 \times (4 - .4)] - .4$

$15 = (4 \times 4) - (4 \div 4)$

$16 = 4 + 4 + 4 + 4$

$17 = (4 \times 4) + (4 \div 4)$

$18 = 4 + 4 + (4 \div .4)$

$19 = [(4 + 4) - .4] \div .4$

$20 = 4 \times [4 + (4 \div 4)]$

Other equations are possible.

. . . . Explanation . . . .

Success hinges on a knowledge of the correct order of operations and seeing interrelationship among numbers.

80
Space Station

Difficulty Level: High
Materials: Paper, pencils

Tell . . . . Show

The figure on the board depicts a space station with square landing pads. Number the landing pads so that each straight line of three connected pads adds up to 9. The numbers you can use are 2¼, 1½, 0, 3, 5¼, 6, 4½, 3¾, ¾.

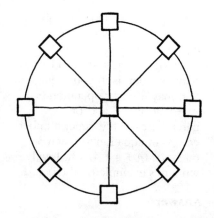

2¼, 1½, 0, 3, 5¼, 6, 4½, 3¾, ¾

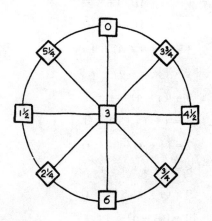

. . . . Explanation . . . .

The set of nine numbers makes a sequence (¾ difference between numbers) which can be placed in a 3-by-3 magic square.

81

Sign Up

Difficulty Level: Medium
Materials: Paper, pencils

Tell . . . . Show

On the board I will place an equation with the operational signs (×, +, ÷, −) missing. You are to complete the equation by filling the correct signs in the boxes. No sign can be used more than once in the same equation. A sample is on the board.

6 ☐ 1 ☐ 3 ☐ 10 = 11

$6 + 1 \times 3 - 10 = 11$

Here are the problems for you to solve:

1. 4 ☐ 2 ☐ 3 ☐ 6 = 5

2. 1 ☐ 8 ☐ 9 ☐ 4 = 0

3. 3 ☐ 4 ☐ 6 ☐ 2 = 40

4. 12 ☐ 4 ☐ 5 ☐ 2 = 16

5. 5 ☐ 7 ☐ 7 ☐ 7 = 4

1. $4 \times 2 + 3 - 6 = 5$

2. $1 + 8 - 9 \times 4 = 0$

3. $3 + 4 \times 6 - 2 = 40$

4. $12 \div 4 + 5 \times 2 = 16$

5. $5 \times 7 - 7 \div 7 = 4$

. . . . Explanation . . . .

Although trial-and-error solutions are most common, some pupils might have an intuitive grasp of the mathematical relationships.

82
Alphabet Antics

Difficulty Level: High
Materials: Papers, pencils

Tell . . . . Show

On the board is a 5-by-5 grid.
Can you fill it up with the letters
A, B, C, D, and E so that no letter
appears twice in any row, in any
column, or in any diagonal?

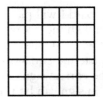

. . . . Explanation . . . .

A student can intuitively solve this problem with trial-and-error thinking. It
is based on magic squares, and it is called a Latin Square. A solution is:

A	B	C	D	E
D	E	A	B	C
B	C	D	E	A
E	A	B	C	D
C	D	E	A	B

83
Bottled Up

Difficulty Level: High
Materials: Paper, pencils

Tell . . . . Show

On a table are 12 bottles with capacities from 1 to 12 ounces. Draw a continuous line separating the bottles into two groups with an equal total of ounces in each group.

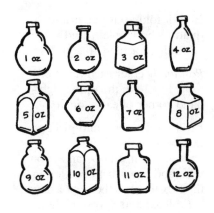

$6 + 10 + 11 + 12 = 39$
$1 + 2 + 3 + 4 + 5 + 7 + 8 + 9 = 39$

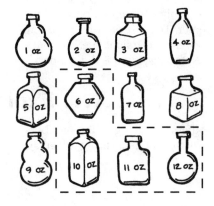

. . . . Explanation . . . .

Mathematical deduction indicates smaller units (bottles) of higher amounts each must be balanced by larger units with smaller capacities. This limits the number of likely combinations and makes a solution possible by trial-and-error manipulation.

84
Numbingo

Difficulty Level: Medium
Materials: Paper, pencils, dice

Tell . . . . Show

Line or fold your paper into quarters horizontally and vertically, forming 16 squares.

Randomly enter each number from 1 to 16 in the upper right-hand corner of each square.

I will roll two dice and place the numbers on the board. You choose any math operation you wish and enter that equation in the box that has the right answer. If I roll a 4 and 3, you might make a 7 (4 + 3), a 1 (4 − 3), or 12 (4 × 3). Only choose one problem to enter. The first person to use four boxes in a straight line calls out "Numbingo" and is the winner.

6	2	14	8
5	10	1	13
11	15	12	3
4	7	16	9

. . . . Explanation . . . .

Strategic placing of the numbers most likely to occur when two dice are rolled confers a strong advantage.

85
Open, Sesame!

Difficulty Level: Medium
Materials: None

Tell . . . . Show

Jane's school locker uses a combination lock that needs the correct three-digit number entered to unlock it. The padlock only uses five digits from 0 to 4. No numeral is used more than once in a combination.

I will call on someone to guess Jane's combination. I'll write the guess on the board, along with some clues. If a digit is completely wrong, meaning it is not part of the combination, I'll mark an "X" in the column for that digit. If a digit is used in the combination, but is in the wrong place, I'll put a question mark in that column. If a number is used in the combination and is in the correct position, I'll mark that column with an asterisk, or star.

Student	Guess	Clues		
		100s	10s	1s
Anne	412	X	?	*
Jack	102	*	X	*
Jill	132	*	*	*

In this example, the combination chosen by the teacher was 132.

. . . . Explanation . . . .

This activity introduces the students to the nuances of inductive reasoning and reinforces understanding of the base 10 place value system. It can be made more difficult for advanced classes by allowing repeated numerals in the combination or adding more digits to the combination.

86
Checkout

Difficulty Level: Medium
Materials: Paper, pencils

Tell . . . . Show

Mrs. Jackson left the supermarket with exactly $1.19 in coins in her purse, with the largest coin a half-dollar. She found to her amazement, in spite of having all these coins, she still couldn't make correct change for a dollar, a half-dollar, a quarter, a dime, or even a nickel. What coins were in her purse?

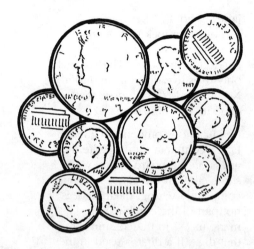

Answer:		
	1 half-dollar	.50
	1 quarter	.25
	4 dimes	.40
	4 pennies	.04
		$1.19

. . . . Explanation . . . .

This money problem involves logical thinking due to the restrictions imposed on making correct change.

87
Triple Threat

Difficulty Level: Medium
Materials: Paper, pencils

Tell . . . . Show

Using every one of the digits from 1 to 9 only once, make an addition problem with its answer like the one on the board. Use only three-digit numbers. See how many you can make.

$$738$$
$$+ 216$$
$$954$$

Some other solutions are:

658	564	192
314	219	384
972	783	576

478	273	259
215	546	614
693	819	873

. . . . Explanation . . . .

The digital sum of the answer is always 18 (in the example on the board 9 + 5 + 4 = 18). Working backwards from this sum, it is easier to generate the addends.

88

Soothsayer

Difficulty Level: Medium
Materials: Paper, pencils

Tell . . . . Show

Write five consecutive numbers
starting with any number from 1
to 100. An example is on the
board.

14, 15, 16, 17, 18

Find the total of your five
numbers.

80

I will ask you for your total and
will tell you the sequence of
numbers you chose.

Divide the total by 5, which will
give you the middle number of
the sequence. Going back two
numbers from this middle number
gives you the first number of the
five-number sequence.

. . . . Explanation . . . .

In any sequence with an odd number of entries, the middle one divides the
whole sequence into two parts and is the average. Dividing the sum by the
number of entries always gives you this average. If the sequence had been
three entries instead of five, you would have divided by 3 to get the middle
number (average).

89
Switcheroo

Difficulty Level: Medium
Materials: None

Tell . . . . Show

On the board are two rows of glasses. Half are filled with chocolate milk. By moving only one glass in the top row, can you make that top row exactly like the bottom row? How can this be done?

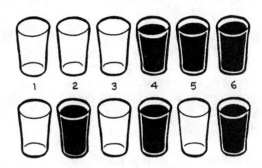

Answer: Pour the #5 glass into the #2 glass and return it to its original position.

. . . . Explanation . . . .

A deadlock develops when you try an inflexible interpretation of the problem. Therefore, a creative element, i.e., pouring, must be introduced into the solution.

90
Multi-Jet

Difficulty Level: High
Materials: Paper, pencils

Tell . . . . Show

I will ask you to get ⅔ of ¾ of certain numbers. One way to do it would be to first find ¾ of the number and then find ⅔ of that answer. For instance, if I give the number 12, you would first find that ¾ of 12 is 9, and then ⅔ of 9 is 6.

¾ of 12 = 9, and ⅔ of 9 = 6.

Now find ⅔ of ¾ of 16.

¾ of 16 = 12, and ⅔ of 12 = 8.

Find ⅔ of ¾ of 24. I will ask one of you to give a number between 1 and 100 that is also a multiple of 4 for all of us to work on using the same procedure. First find ¾ of the number and then find ⅔ of the answer. You will try to get the answer before I write it on a piece of paper and put it in my pocket.

¾ of 24 = 18, and ⅔ of 18 = 12.

The answer will *always* be half of the given number!

. . . . Explanation . . . .

Three-quarters of any number on can be shown as follows:

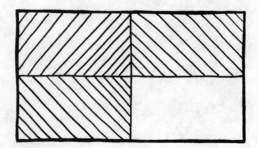

Three-quarters of this figure refers to the shaded parts and it can be seen that two of these shaded parts is one-half of the original square or number. The mathematical equation for this is:

$$2/3 \times 3/4 = 6/12 = 1/2$$

91
Fun and Games

Difficulty Level: High
Materials: Paper, pencils

Tell . . . . Show

Sharon went to a game store and bought a chess set and a book, which together cost $12.50. The chess set cost $2.50 more than the book. How much did each cost?

Chess set	$ 7.50
Book	$ 5.00
	$12.50

. . . . Explanation . . . .

This seems like a simple subtraction problem ($12.50 − $2.50 = ?), but actually it involves an algebraic solution.

92
Computique

Difficulty Level: Medium
Materials: Paper, pencils

Tell . . . . Show

I will call on a pupil to give me a two-place number, and I will multiply it by 11 in my computer brain and get the answer before anyone in the class can figure it out.

The digits of any two-place numbers are the outside numbers in the answer. The middle number in the answer is found by adding these two digits. So, with 45, the outside numbers in the answer are 4 and 5 and the middle is the sum of 4 and 5 (9). Therefore, 45 × 11 = 495. However, when the two digits add up to more than nine, carry a one to the first outside number. With 75 × 11, 7 + 5 = 12, so the one is added to the 7 and the answer is 825.

. . . . Explanation . . . .

This is a shortcut method involving place value manipulation.

93
Squaresville

Difficulty Level: Medium
Materials: Paper, pencils

Tell . . . . Show

I will call on a pupil to give me any two-place number ending in a 5, and I will multiply it by itself (square it) in my head and get the answer before anyone in the class can do it on paper.

Take the first digit of the number and multiply by the next higher digit and then place "25" at the end of that answer. For example, with 65 × 65, take the 6 and multiply it by 7 (42) and place 25 after it (4225).

. . . . Explanation . . . .

This is a shortcut method involving the place value manipulation.

94
Omni-Fun

Difficulty Level: High
Materials: Paper, pencils

Tell . . . . Show

Using every one of the digits
from 1 to 9 once, make up a
multiplication problem with its
answer. A sample problem is on
the board.

$$\begin{array}{r} 297 \\ \times\ 18 \\ \hline 5346 \end{array}$$

Some other solutions:

$$\begin{array}{r} 159 \\ \times\ 48 \\ \hline 7632 \end{array}$$

$$\begin{array}{r} 157 \\ \times\ 28 \\ \hline 4396 \end{array}$$

$$\begin{array}{r} 198 \\ \times\ 27 \\ \hline 5346 \end{array}$$

. . . . Explanation . . . .

Trial and error will provide solutions.

95
Full House

Difficulty Level: Medium
Materials: Paper, pencils

Tell . . . . Show

Using every one of the digits 1 to
5 once, devise a multiplication
equation (problem and answer).

$13 \times 4 = 52$

. . . . Explanation . . . .

The basic requirement to complete this task is to have a knowledge of the
multiplication table.

96
Robin Hood

Difficulty Level: Medium
Materials: Paper, pencils

Tell . . . . Show

I have drawn a bull's-eye on the board. You are Robin Hood, and I will ask you to shoot a particular score using the fewest possible arrows. For example, a score of 7 would have to hit the 4, 2, and 1 rings with 3 arrows.

A. Shoot a 25
B. Shoot a 19
C. Shoot a 47

Answer:

A. 16, 8, 1
B. 16, 2, 1
C. 32, 8, 4, 2, 1

. . . . Explanation . . . .

Any whole number up to 63 can be formed on this target. Each number is a power of 2, which allows any whole number to be written that is one less than the next succeeding power. On this target, the next succeeding power would be 64.

97
Ultra

Difficulty Level: Medium
Materials: Paper, pencils

Tell . . . . Show

Using all the digits from 1 to 5
once, create two multiplicands
that provide the largest possible
answer.

$$\begin{array}{r} 431 \\ \times\ \ 52 \\ \hline 22{,}412 \end{array}$$

. . . . Explanation . . . .

Pupils must understand that larger numbers must be used in the higher
place value positions.

98

Caboose

Difficulty Level: High
Materials: Paper, pencils

Tell . . . . Show

I will call on a pupil to write a three-digit number on the board. The class will try to beat me in figuring out a digit to attach at the end of this number in order to make the whole four-digit number exactly divisible by 9.

Add the individual digits of the three-digit number and subtract this total from the next multiple of nine. This subtraction answer is the number you need to attach to the end of the given three-digit number.

Example:
471 = 4 + 7 + 1 = 12.

The next multiple of 9 is 18, and 12 from 18 leaves 6. Attaching the 6 to the end of 471 makes it 4716, which is now divisible by 9 (4716 ÷ 9 = 524). If the three digits add up to an exact multiple of 9, you can attach either 0 or 9 to the three-digit number.

. . . . Explanation . . . .

Adding individual digits is the standard divisibility test for nine.

99
Hide 'n' Seek

Difficulty Level: High
Materials: Paper, pencils

Tell . . . . Show

I have written an addition
problem on the board with an
incorrect answer. You can make
this answer correct by removing
certain digits in the problem.
On your paper, show how the
addition problem should look in
order to get this answer.

```
 111
 333
 555
 777
 999
─────
1111
```

```
 111
   3

   7
  99
────
1111
```

. . . . Explanation . . . .

This exercise depends on knowledge of our numeration system and the
ability to see combinations that equal 11.

100
Candy Cutter

Difficulty Level: Low
Materials: None

Tell . . . . Show

Tim cut his licorice stick into 12 equal pieces and took five seconds to make each cut. If he started cutting at 3:17 p.m., when would he finish?

3:17:55 (55 seconds after 3:17)

. . . . Explanation . . . .

It takes only 11 cuts to make 12 equal pieces, as shown in this diagram:

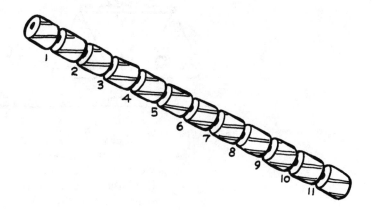

101
Ruby Roundup

Difficulty Level: Medium
Materials: Paper, pencils

Tell . . . . Show

A jeweler bought nine rubies and learned that one of them was a fake that would weigh less than the real ones. How could he find the fake ruby with only two weighings of the rubies on his balance scale?

First he must divide the rubies into three piles of three rubies each. He then picks two piles to weigh on the scale.

1.

If either pile A or B goes up, then the fake ruby is on the side that went up. If the scale remains level, the fake ruby is off the scale in pile C. In any case, one weighing locates the pile having the fake ruby.

2.

Take the pile that has the fake ruby and weigh two of the three rubies. The side that goes up has the fake ruby, or, if the scale stays level, the ruby off the scale is fake.

············· **Explanation** ···············

The ability to use inferential thinking in a sequential fashion leads to the correct conclusion.

102
7-11

Difficulty Level: High
Materials: Paper, pencils

Tell . . . . Show

A cook must boil rice for exactly 15 minutes, using a 7-minute hourglass and an 11-minute hourglass. How can the cook do this? Illustrate your solution.

Start both hourglasses together with the rice off the fire.

When all sand in the 7-minute hourglass is on the bottom, place the rice on the fire. There will still be 4 minutes of sand left in the top of the 11-minute hourglass.

When these 4 minutes have passed, all the sand will be on the bottom of both hourglasses, and the rice has been boiling for 4 minutes. Turn the 11-minute timer over. It will start again and this 11 minutes plus the previous 4 will total 15 minutes boiling time.

.... Explanation..............

This exercise is an adaptation of a famous problem involving creatively arranging known elements into a new configuration.

103
Weigh Out

Difficulty Level: High
Materials: Paper, pencils

Tell . . . . Show

Farmer Jones uses a balance scale to weigh any produce from 1 to 40 pounds. He needs only four weights, which he uses in various combinations. These weights are 1, 3, 9, and 27 pounds, which can be placed on either side of the scale. Illustrate how he can weigh out the following amounts of produce:

A. 12 pounds

B. 37 pounds

C. 25 pounds

D. 32 pounds

E. 20 pounds

·············· **Explanation**··············

This problem is a form of a Bachet weight puzzle based on the ternary (base-three) numeration system.

104
Ship Ahoy

Difficulty Level: Medium
Materials: None

Tell . . . . Show

A ship at anchor has a rope ladder 12 feet long hanging from it. The rungs on the ladder are 1½ feet apart with the first rung touching the water. If the tide rises at 6 inches per hour, how long would it be before the first five rungs are under water?

They will never be under water because the ship rises with the tide along with the attached ladder.

. . . . Explanation . . . .

This solution is an application of the buoyancy principle and the numerical information is irrelevant.

105
Alphabet Soup

Difficulty Level: Medium
Materials: None

Tell . . . . Show

On the board is a picture of two
bowls of alphabet soup. The
letters in each bowl belong
together because they share a
certain characteristic in common.
Place each of the letters S, T, U,
and V in the correct bowl and be
ready to give a good reason for
choosing that bowl.

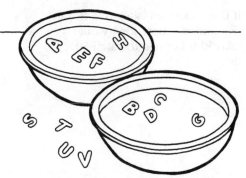

Answer: T and V should be
grouped with A, E, F, and H. S
and U belong with B, C, D, and
G.

. . . . Explanation . . . .

The letters in the top bowl can all be formed with straight line strokes while
the others require curved strokes. This problem involves categorical
thinking based on perceptual cues.

106
Scaley Tale

Difficulty Level: High
Materials: None

Tell . . . . Show

If five fishermen catch five fish in five minutes, how long would it take 50 fishermen to catch 50 fish?

Answer: Five minutes

. . . . Explanation . . . .

You must assume it takes each fisherman 5 minutes to catch a single fish. Therefore, the time element would never change regardless of how many fishermen and fish are involved. This is an example of axiomatic reasoning.

107
Razzle Dazzle

Difficulty Level: Medium
Materials: None

Tell . . . . Show

A quarterback's brother died and left all his money to his only brother. However, the quarterback never received any of this money even though it was legally paid out. How could this happen?

The quarterback was a girl!

. . . . Explanation . . . .

Difficulties in figuring out the answer are related to stereotyped linking between sexes and "appropriate" jobs leading to a false assumption, i.e., quarterbacks *must* be men.

108
Lunch Bunch

Difficulty Level: Low
Materials: None

Tell .... Show

The principal asked a teacher how many kids were still in the lunch line. The teacher replied, "There is one kid in front of two kids, a kid behind two kids, and a kid between two kids." How many kids were in the lunch line?

Answer: Three kids

.... Explanation ....

This question demonstrates order relationships and shows three different ways of describing each position (kid).

109
Gumball

Difficulty Level: Medium
Materials: None

Tell . . . . Show

Jack and Jill went up the hill to get gumballs from a penny machine. The machine had 30 red gumballs and 30 green gumballs. If they got one gumball for each penny they put in the machine, how many pennies would they spend before they could be certain of sharing two gumballs of the same color?

Answer: Three pennies

. . . . Explanation . . . .

After the second penny, Jack and Jill would have either: (a) two gumballs of the same color or (b) two gumballs of different colors. A third penny would deliver a gumball that had to match one of the colors.

110
Bye-Bye Birdie

Difficulty Level: Low
Materials: None

Tell . . . . Show

Dolly and Dotty were playing badminton in their backyard when the birdie fell into a hole. It was so deep they couldn't reach it by hand or with any stick. How did they finally get the birdie back?

Answer: They flooded the hole with water, and the birdie floated to the top.

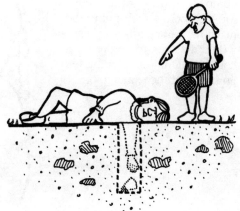

. . . . Explanation . . . .

Flexible thinking and a knowledge of the physical principle of buoyancy solves this problem.

III
Arabian Nights

Difficulty Level: High
Materials: Three black markers, three white markers, three boxes

Tell .... Show

When Ali Baba was traveling in Arabia, he was faced with this problem. The sultan showed him three boxes that each concealed two pearls. He was told that one box contained two white pearls (WW), one had two black pearls (BB), and the third box had one black and one white pearl (BW). The boxes were marked BB, WW, and BW, but each box was marked incorrectly. The sultan ordered Ali Baba to label the boxes correctly, allowing him to take only *one* pearl from *any* box he wished. If he succeeded, he would keep the six pearls, but if he failed, his head would be chopped off. You are to figure out the only sure way for him to solve his problem and be prepared to explain it.

A picture of the sultan's boxes is on the board. They are also on my desk.

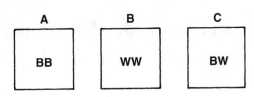

Ali Baba must choose a pearl from the box marked BW, which must be mislabeled. If he takes out a black pearl, then the other pearl must also be black because the only other choice would be WW, which is impossible since he drew a black.

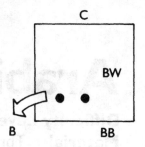

On the other hand, if he draws a white, then the box must be WW. If white were drawn, we know that this box should be labeled WW. Let's assume it's the white pearl that was drawn and therefore the box should be labeled WW.

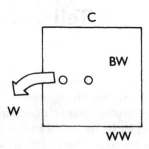

By taking the WW label from the middle box to its correct placement on the box on the right, we leave the middle box with no label. Since we know the left-hand box is mislabeled, its label belongs to the middle box because it's the only place for it. The BW label is left for the left-hand box. The correct labels are as follows:

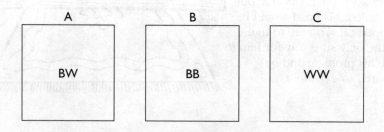

·············· **Explanation**··············

This problem is a classical case of using deductive reasoning to solve a logic situation.

112
Antricks

Difficulty Level: Medium
Materials: None

Tell . . . . Show

An ant, starting from the 12-inch end, crawls along the edge of a ruler. It covers half the distance in 12 seconds. How much longer would it take the ant to reach the 1-inch mark?

Answer: 10 seconds

. . . . Explanation . . . .

The diagram shows there are six intervals from the 12-inch to the 6-inch mark, and since the ant averages two seconds per interval, it takes a total of 12 seconds to cover the distance. However, from the 6-inch to the 1-inch mark there are only five intervals, and at the same speed, the ant would take 10 seconds to cover this distance.

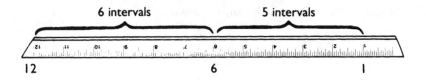

6 intervals   5 intervals

12   6   1

113
Big Ben

Difficulty Level: High
Materials: Paper, pencils

Tell . . . . Show

Big Ben, London's largest clock,
signals the time with loud bongs.
If it takes three seconds to make
three bongs at three o'clock, how
many seconds will it take to
make six bongs at six o'clock?

Answer: 7½ seconds

. . . . Explanation . . . .

The "bonging" for three o'clock can be shown as follows:

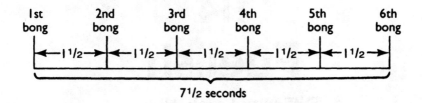

7¹/₂ seconds

The first bong accounts for the interval from 1 to 2, the second bong accounts for the interval from 2 to 3, which ends with the third bong. Therefore, the three seconds have to be divided in half since there are only two intervals for the three bongs, averaging 1½ seconds per interval.

At six o'clock, there are five intervals, totaling 7½ seconds, as shown:

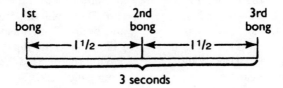

3 seconds

114
Fuelish

Difficulty Level: High
Materials: Paper, pencils

Tell . . . . Show

A motorcyclist ran out of gas on a small road off the highway and needed exactly 2 gallons for his tank. A helpful trucker had two empty cans that could hold 5 gallons and 8 gallons. How could the biker use these cans to measure out the needed 2 gallons? Illustrate your answer.

Answer: First fill the 5-gallon can and empty it into the 8-gallon can. Then refill the 5-gallon can and pour as much as you can (3 gallons) into the 8-gallon can, leaving the needed 2 gallons in the 5-gallon can.

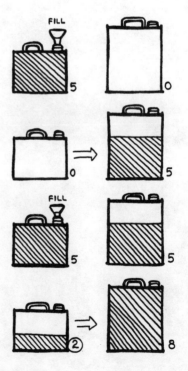

. . . . Explanation . . . .

This is a time-honored decanting problem based on divisibility analysis.

115
Wall Ball

Difficulty Level: Medium
Materials: None

Tell . . . . Show

There are 24 players entered in a racquetball singles tournament in which each loser is eliminated. How many matches must be played to determine who wins the cup for first place?

Answer: 23 matches

. . . . Explanation . . . .

Each time a match is played, one player is eliminated. After 23 matches are played, only the winner remains. Diagrammatically it can be shown as follows:

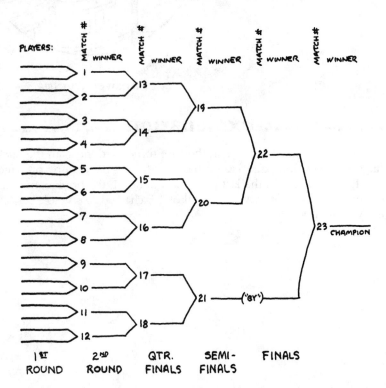

116
Bookworm

Difficulty Level: High
Materials: Paper, pencils

Tell . . . . Show

A hungry bookworm is eating its way through an encyclopedia set on a library bookshelf. Each book cover is ¼ inch thick, and the pages are 1 inch thick. If the bookworm starts on page 1 of Volume I and eats its way on a straight path to the last page of Volume III, how far will it have traveled?

Answer: 2 inches

. . . . Explanation . . . .

When books are placed on a shelf, they are turned around with the back bindings showing, and page 1 is on the right-hand side. Starting on page 1, Volume I, and ending on the last page of Volume III, the bookworm will travel through four book covers (a total of 1 inch) and one whole set of pages (Volume II = 1 inch).

117
Link Think

Difficulty Level: Medium
Materials: Paper, pencils

Tell .... Show

Andy has five sections of chain he can link together to make a bike chain. Each section has three links, as shown on the board. If it cost 5¢ to cut open a link and 10¢ to weld it shut, what is the least amount of money it would cost to join the five sections?

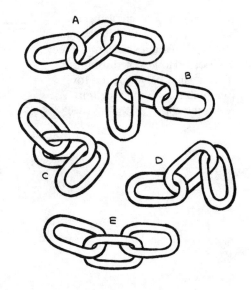

Answer: 45¢

.... Explanation ....

Instead of cutting all the end links, cut *each* link in Section E so you have three open links. One of these links will join Sections A and B, the second link joins Sections B and C, while the third link joins Sections C and D, and weld all three links. This makes three cuts (15¢) and three weldings (30¢).

118
Day Crawler

Difficulty Level: Medium
Materials: None

Tell . . . . Show

A worm trying to climb up the steep, slippery wall of a dam 20 feet high manages to climb 5 feet each day. However, during the night it slips back 4 feet. How long will it take the worm to reach the top?

Answer: 16 days

. . . . Explanation . . . .

The worm makes a net gain of 1 foot for each 24-hour day. After 15 days, it will be 5 feet short of the top of the 20-foot high dam. The 5-foot move during the 16th day puts it over the top.

119
Jaws

Difficulty Level: Medium
Materials: None

Tell . . . . Show

A stranger in an isolated village had a throbbing toothache and had to decide which of the town's two dentists should take care of it. He saw that one dentist had a beautiful modern office with new equipment, and this dentist's teeth showed visible evidence of excellent dental work. The other dentist had a plain office with old-fashioned equipment, and his teeth showed the effects of poor dental work. Which dentist should the stranger choose and why?

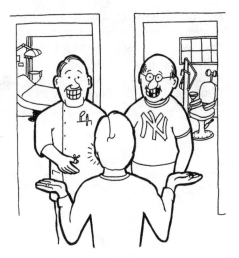

The stranger should choose the dentist who had the plain office and poor teeth.

. . . . Explanation . . . .

This logic situation is a version of Russell's Paradox. Dentists cannot work on their own teeth, therefore each showed the effects of the other one's work because there are only two dentists in town.

120
Watermelon

Difficulty Level: Low
Materials: None

Tell . . . . Show

Sid and Sylvia pooled their
money to buy a watermelon.
They wanted to slice it exactly in
half and be sure that they were
both satisfied with their share.
What would be the fairest way to
do this?

The fairest way is to have one
person cut the melon while the
other gets first choice.

. . . . Explanation . . . .

According to the Bible, a similar dilemma was solved by King Solomon.
Since the other person gets first choice, the person cutting the melon will
take care to cut it in half as accurately as possible.

121
Reunion

Difficulty Level: High
Materials: None

Tell .... Show

At a class reunion, Mr. Blue, Mr. Gray, and Mr. White sat together. The man with the blue shirt said, "Have any of you noticed that although the colors of our shirts are the same as our names, none of us is wearing a shirt that is the same color as his own name?" "Yes, you're right," answered Mr. White. What color shirt was each man wearing?

Mr. Gray—blue shirt
Mr. White—gray shirt
Mr. Blue—white shirt

.... Explanation ....

Since each man's name cannot match the color of his shirt, the man with the blue shirt who was talking must be Mr. Gray or Mr. White. However, Mr. White answered him, so the only name remaining for the blue-shirted man is Mr. Gray. Mr. White cannot be wearing the white shirt, and since the blue shirt is being worn by Mr. Gray, this leaves the gray shirt for Mr. White. The remaining match has to be Mr. Blue with the white shirt. This logic riddle requires syllogistic reasoning.

122
Sandwich

Difficulty Level: Medium
Materials: None

Tell . . . . Show

What arithmetic symbol can we place between 20 and 5 to give an answer larger than 4 but smaller than 25?

$$20 \quad 5 =$$
Solution: $20 - 5 = 15$

What arithmetic symbol can we place between 8 and 9 to give an answer larger than 8 but smaller than 9?

$$8 \quad 9 =$$
Solution: $8 . 9 = 8.9$

. . . . Explanation . . . .

It can quickly be seen that the operational symbols (+, −, ×, ÷) do not solve the second problem and some other symbol is needed.

123
Down Under

Difficulty Level: High
Materials: Paper, pencils

Tell . . . . Show

A sheep rancher in Australia gets 1½ pounds of wool from 1½ sheep in 1½ days. How many pounds of wool will he get from 6 sheep in 7 days?

Answer: 28 pounds of wool

. . . . Explanation . . . .

Since he gets 1½ pounds from 1½ sheep in 1½ days, doubling the sheep would double the amount of wool in the same period of time, i.e., three pounds from three sheep in 1½ days (Row B in the chart). Reducing the time to one day is cutting the time by ⅓ (1 day is ⅔ of 1½) and would reduce production by ⅓, giving 2 pounds of wool, i.e., ⅔ of 3 pounds = 2 (Row C). Doubling the number of sheep would double the wool production in the same amount of time (Row D). Multiplying the number of days by 7 would also multiply the wool production by 7, giving 28 pounds (Row E).

	Sheep	Wool	Days
A	1½	1½	1½
B	3	3	1½
C	3	2	1
D	6	4	1
E	6	28	7

124
Boutique

Difficulty Level: Medium
Materials: None

Tell . . . . Show

Two mothers and two daughters went shopping together. Each bought a dress for $50. How much did they spend altogether?

$150

. . . . Explanation . . . .

Only three dresses were bought, since the women who went shopping were three members of the same family, consisting of a grandmother, mother, and daughter. The following diagram shows how this order relationship can be seen as 2 mothers and 2 daughters:

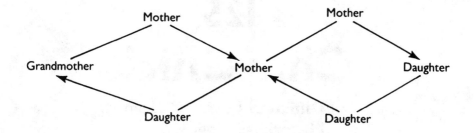

This problem is an example of equivalence relationship.

125
Chic Chick

Difficulty Level: Medium
Materials: None

Tell . . . . Show

During a blackout, Ms. Astor went to her drawer to find a pair of earrings and a pair of stockings. In the drawer she had three pairs of earrings mixed together and nine pairs of black or brown stockings thrown together. Drawing one at a time, how many earrings and stockings must she take out of her drawer in order to be certain she has a matching pair of each?

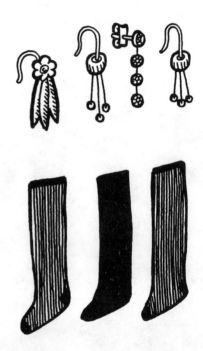

Answer: Four earrings and three stockings

. . . . Explanation . . . .

She could draw three different times without having a matched pair of earrings. The fourth pick would guarantee an earring to match one of the previous three.

She could draw two times without having two matching stockings. The third pick would ensure a stocking to match one of the other two.

126
United Nations

Difficulty Level: High
Materials: Paper, pencils

Tell . . . . Show

A Frenchman married an Italian woman. They both had children from their first marriages. After they had been married 12 years, they had a family of 10 children in all. The children she had from her first marriage spoke only Italian, and the children he had from his first marriage spoke only French. If they each had eight of their own from both marriages, and the children born after their marriage to each other spoke only English, how many English-speaking children did they have?

Answer: Six English-speaking children

. . . . Explanation . . . .

Since from their combined total of 10 children, he had eight children from both of his marriages, this leaves two children as exclusively hers from her previous marriages. And, since from their 10 children she also had eight from both her marriages, this leaves two children as exclusively his from his previous marriage. Therefore, already having four children between them when they got married, they had another six children to bring the total to 10. These six spoke English. This might be illustrated with a Venn diagram as follows:

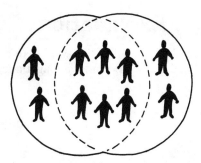

127
Skateboard

Difficulty Level: High
Materials: None

Tell . . . . Show

Mike decided to skateboard from his home to visit his friend Paul. Three miles away from home his skateboard broke down, and he had to walk the remaining two miles to Paul's place. He couldn't repair the skateboard and had to walk all the way back home. How many miles *more* did he walk than he rode? Make sure you can explain or illustrate your answer.

He walked 4 miles more than he rode. This can be illustrated as follows:

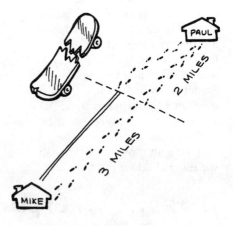

It can be shown that between his home and the breakdown point, he walked and rode the same distance (3 miles). From the breakdown point to Paul's home he had to walk both ways, which totals the extra 4 miles.

. . . . Explanation . . . .

This verbal problem involves analytical thinking more than computational skills. A sophisticated analysis could render an algebraic solution.

128
Shake, Rattle, & Roll

Difficulty Level: High
Materials: None

Tell . . . . Show

A gambler bought seven large boxes of dice with each die weighing exactly 10 grams. However, a friend tipped him off that one of the boxes had dice in which each die in the box was lighter than the dice in the other boxes by 1 gram. With just one weighing, how could he determine the lighter box?

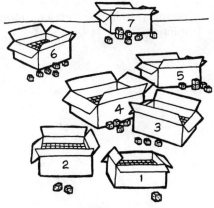

Take one die from Box #1, take two from Box #2, take 3 from Box #3 and continue until you have taken 7 from Box #7. Weigh these dice together, and they should weigh 280 grams.

If, for example, Box #5, contained the lighter dice, the total would not be 280 but 275 since five lighter dice came from that box. The same reasoning would hold true for any of the boxes.

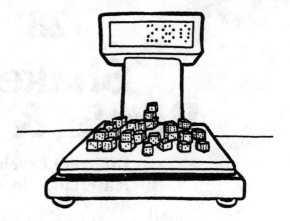

$\cdots\cdots\cdots\cdots$ **Explanation** $\cdots\cdots\cdots\cdots$

Solving this puzzle is dependent upon using the principles of deductive reasoning.

129
Crisscross

Difficulty Level: High
Materials: Paper, pencils

Tell . . . . Show

A farmer going on a trip with a squirrel, acorns, and a fox had to cross a river in a boat in which he couldn't take more than one of them with him each time he crossed. Since he had to leave two of them together on one side of the river or the other, how could he plan the crossings so that nothing gets eaten, and they all get across the river safely? Try to illustrate your crossings.

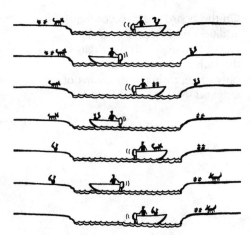

. . . . Explanation . . . .

To solve this problem, you must realize that the fox won't eat the acorns but will eat the squirrel, and the squirrel will eat the acorns. The farmer has to carry one of the three with him in the canoe to avoid this problem.

130
Take Route 666

Difficulty Level: Medium
Materials: Papers, pencils

Tell . . . . Show

On the board are two column addition problems. Fill in the empty squares with the digits 0 through 8, using each number only once, to make the sums of 666 and 999.

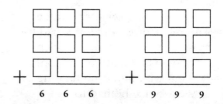

Two solutions (note that some of the digits can be interchanged):

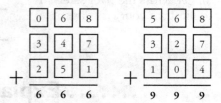

. . . . Explanation . . . .

Through trial-and-error analysis a student will be able to solve these problems. A turtle and a snail are 300 inches away from each other on a narrow path.

131
Traveling Ant-ics

Difficulty Level: High
Materials: Paper, pencils

Tell . . . . Show

They travel directly towards each other, with the turtle going 4 inches per minute and the snail 1 inch per minute. When they're 100 inches apart, the turtle almost steps on an ant, which scurries away directly towards the snail. Upon reaching the snail, it turns around and races back towards the turtle.

The ant continues going back and forth between the two at a speed of 10 inches per minute. When the turtle and snail meet and squash the poor ant, how many inches will it have run? The ant will have run 200 inches.

. . . . Explanation . . . .

The turtle and the snail are closing the gap at a combined speed of 5 inches per minute (turtle 4 inches per minute + snail 1 inch per minute = 5 inches per minute). When they are 100 inches apart, it will take them 20 minutes more to meet, since 100 inches of distance divided by a combined speed of 5 inches per minute equals 20 minutes. The ant, going at a speed of 10 inches per minute, will travel a total of 200 inches (10 inches per minute × 20 minutes = 200 inches). Any other figures are irrelevant to the solution.

132
Calendar Trick

Difficulty Level: Medium
Materials: Calculators, calendar,
papers, pencils

Tell . . . . Show

On the board is a calendar. I want
a volunteer to draw a box around
any group of nine numbers that
form a 3-by-3 square. I will face
away from the board so I don't
see the square. Tell me only the
first number in the square. Use
your calculators to find the sum
of these numbers, while I add
them in my head. We'll race to
find who can find the sum of
these nine numbers first.
What is your final answer?

. . . . Explanation . . . .

As an example, we'll solve this 3-by-3 square:

$$\begin{array}{ccc} 4 & 5 & 6 \\ 11 & 12 & 13 \\ 18 & 19 & 20 \end{array}$$

The teacher is told the first number, 4, adds 8 to it to get the middle
number, and multiplies this number by 9 for a sum of 108. In this 3-by-3
square, 12 is the middle, or average, number, and 9 × 12 = 108. In effect,
the middle number times 9 always equals the sum.

133
Birthday Magic

Difficulty Level: High
Materials: Calculators, papers, pencils

Tell . . . . Show

I can guess your birthday. As I give you the following directions, enter them in your calculator one at a time.

1. Enter the number that stands for the month in which you were born.
2. Double it.
3. Add 6.
4. Multiply by 50.
5. Add the day of your birth.
6. Subtract 365.

What is your final answer?

January	February	March
1	**2**	**3**
April	May	June
4	**5**	**6**
July	August	September
7	**8**	**9**
October	November	December
10	**11**	**12**

Add 65 to the final answer to get the student's birthday. For example, if the student's answer is 136, add 65 for sum of 201. In order to change 201 into a birthday, put a slash between the tens and hundreds place. Therefore 201 becomes 2/01. The student's birthday is February 1.

. . . . Explanation . . . .

Using the distributive property of multiplication, you are multiplying the month by 100 to get it in the hundreds place, then adding 300; then you add the date to get it in the tens and ones place, and then subtract 365. You add the 65 to balance the addition and subtraction.

134
Crystal Ball

Difficulty Level: High
Materials: Calculators, three dice, papers, pencils

Tell . . . . Show

I will call on volunteers to do simple calculations on their calculators and write their results on the board while I face away from the board.

1. Jane, roll three dice.

3, 1, 5

2. John, multiply the top number on the first die by two.

$3 \times 2 = 6$

3. Bill, add 5 to John's answer.

$6 + 5 = 11$

4. Maria, multiply Bill's result by 5.

$11 \times 5 = 55$

5. Jamal, add the top number on the second die to Maria's total.

$1 + 55 = 56$

6. Vicki, multiply Jamal's answer by 10.

$56 \times 10 = 560$

7. Casper, add the top number on the third die to Vicki's answer.

$5 + 560 = 565$

8. Bobbie, subtract 3 from Casper's result.

$565 - 3 = 562$

What is your final answer?

562

The numbers on the dice are 3, 1, and 5.

. . . . Explanation . . . .

The teacher subtracts 247 from the final answer of 562 for an answer of 315. The 3 in the answer is the 1st die; the 1 is the 2nd die, and the 5 is the 3rd die.

135
Address Book

Difficulty Level: High
Materials: Calculators, papers, pencils

Tell . . . . Show

I will give you the following directions. Enter them one at a time into your calculator. When you tell me your final answer, I will be able to determine your street address.

1. Enter your street address.
2. Add 5.
3. Multiply by 2.
4. Add 9.
5. Multiply by 3.
6. Subtract 57.

What is your final answer?

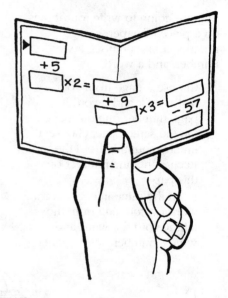

Using a calculator, the teacher divides the final answer by 6. For example, if a student's answer is 1584, the teacher divides it by 6 for an address of 264.

. . . . Explanation . . . .

This problem illustrates the distributive property of multiplication and division over addition and subtraction.

136
Undercover

Difficulty Level: High
Materials: Calculators, papers, pencils

Tell . . . . Show

You are going to write four things on a piece of paper: a page number, a line number, a word number, and a word.

1. Choose a page from your math book and record its page number on your paper.

   Page number: 115

2. On the same page, choose a line by counting from the top. Record the line number on this paper.

   Line number: 11

3. From the same line, choose a word by counting from the left. Record the word and the word's number on the paper.

   Word number: 6

   Word name: Departure

Follow these directions, entering them one at a time in your calculator.

1. Enter 201.
2. Multiply this number by your page number.
3. Add your line number.
4. Add 12.
5. Subtract your page number.
6. Add your line number.
7. Multiply by 5.
8. Add 5.
9. Multiply by 10.
10. Add 16
11. Add your word number.
12. Subtract 666
13. Press the equal (=) key.

What is your final answer?

The student gives the teacher his or her final answer. Using the math book, the teacher then tells the student his or her secret word.

·············· Explanation ···············

In this case, the final answer is 1151106. The first three digits, 115. is the page number, the next two digits, 11, is the line number, and the last two digits, 06, is the position of the word. Therefore, the teacher turns to page 115, goes to line 11, counts over to the 6th word, and calls out the secret word, "departure."

The calculation involves the following: $[(201 \times \text{page} + 12 - \text{page} + \text{line}) \times 5 + 5] \times 10 + 16 + \text{word number} - 666 = \text{page, line, word.}$

137

What's My Secret?

Difficulty Level: Medium
Materials: Calculators, papers, pencils

Tell . . . . Show

Follow these directions by entering them one at a time in your calculator.

The student gives the teacher his or her final answer. The teacher then tells the student his or her secret number.

1. Enter a number between 10 and 100.

   35

2. Subtract your favorite one-digit number.

   −7

3. Multiply it by 9.

   ×9

4. Add your original number.

   +35

5. Press the equal (=) key.

   287

What is your final answer?

. . . . Explanation . . . .

In this example, the final answer is 287. Take the first two digits 28 and add it to the last digit 7 (28+7). This give a sum of 35, the secret number. The calculations involve: (number – one-digit number) × 9 + number.

138
Triple Play

Difficulty Level: Medium
Materials: Calculators, papers, pencils

Tell . . . . Show

On the board, I have written six rows of numbers. The first three rows are in ascending order from 1 to 9, while the last three are in descending order from 9 to 1.

Starting on the left, enter the first row of numbers and press the + key at the end. Continue this procedure for each subsequent row.

Now press the 3 key, followed by the equal (=) key.

What is your final answer?

```
1 2 3 4 5 6 7 8 9
1 2 3 4 5 6 7 8 9
1 2 3 4 5 6 7 8 9
9 8 7 6 5 4 3 2 1
9 8 7 6 5 4 3 2 1
9 8 7 6 5 4 3 2 1
```

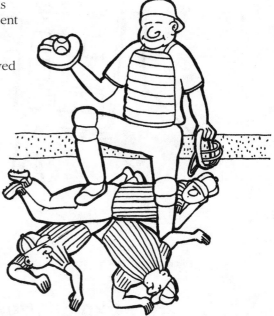

. . . . Explanation . . . .

The sum is always 3,333,333,333, because pairing 1 to 9 with 9 to 1 gives 1,111,111,110. Doing this three times gives you 3,333,333,330 and adding 3 gives you the desired sum.

139
Multi-Math

Difficulty Level: Medium
Materials: Paper, pencils, calculators

Tell . . . . Show

Using seven different digits in the squares, make a correct multiplication equation. There are several different solutions. See how many you can find.

Two possible solutions:

$435 \times 2 = 870$
$176 \times 3 = 528$

. . . . Explanation . . . .

This computational activity requires extensive trial-and-error methodology and is an excellent example of where calculator usage is most beneficial.

Index

About the authors

Dr. Richard M. Sharp is a professor of elementary education at California State University, Northridge. He holds an Ed.D. in mathematics education from Boston University. Dr. Seymour Metzner is a professor emeritus at the Northridge campus of California State University. Drs. Sharp and Metzner are coauthors (with Vicki F. Sharp) of *Scribble Scrabble: Ready-in-a-Minute Math Games* (McGraw-Hill, 1995).